CONQUER WITH CHRIST

CONQUER WITH CHRIST

OVERCOMING ADVERSITIES
THROUGH
THE WORD OF GOD

Marolyn Madison-Evans

Conquer with Christ   Marolyn Madison-Evans

Conquer with Christ   Marolyn Madison-Evans

CONQUER WITH CHRIST
Overcoming Adversities Through The Word of God

Copyright © 2018 by Marolyn Madison-Evans

All rights reserved. No part of this publication may be reproduced or transmitted in any form or by any means – electronic, mechanical, photocopying, recording or otherwise without the prior written consent of the Publisher. The only exception is brief quotations in printed reviews.

Unless otherwise identified, Scripture quotations are from the King James Version of the Bible.

Scripture quotations identified NIV are from the New International Version. Holy Bible. NIV Copyright © 1973, 1978, 1984, 2011 by Biblical, Inc. Used by permission. All rights reserved worldwide.

Scripture quotations identified NKJV are from the New King James Version of the Bible. Copyright © 1979, 1980, 1982 by Thomas, Nelson, Inc. Used by permission. All rights reserved.

Scripture quotations identified ESV are from the English Standard Version. Bible Gateway. Web. Copyright © 25 Oct 2012. Used by permission. All rights reserved.

Published by Marolyn Madison-Evans
P.O. Box 18223
Pensacola, Florida 32523-8223
www.marolynevans.com

Library of Congress Control Number: 2018957042

ISBN-13: 978-1-7327766-0-9
Printed in the United States of America

Table of Contents

Dedication 7

Acknowledgements 8

Preface………………………………………..……..10

Chapter 1 Overcoming Addictions. ………………….11

Chapter 2 Overcoming Depression……………..…. 18

Chapter 3 Managing Anger……………………………32

Chapter 4 Suicide Prevention………………………….40

Chapter 5 Domestic Violence & Rape………………….52

Chapter 6 Issues Impacting Women ……………….62

Chapter 7 Issues impacting Men………………………68

Chapter 8 Love, Sex & Marriage ……………………..79

Chapter 9 Single Living ………………………………99

Chapter 10 Bullying …………………………………106

Chapter 11 Peer Pressure………………….……. ……115

Chapter 12 Salvation and the church…..……………122

Invitation to FMC……………………………...140

Five Church Fellowship………………………………141

A Prayer: By Helen Madison……………………142

References……………………………………...143

Dedication

This book is dedicated to my late beloved sister Sophia L. Madison. Sophia, may you continue to Rest In Peace, knowing that being absent from the body is to be present with the LORD! You will always be loved and your sweet memories will be cherished forever. We love you and we miss you greatly!

To my beloved son Alan V. Evans and my twin grandsons Ali C. Evans and Aki C. Evans. Thank you all for your unwavering love and support toward me. You all are the wind beneath my wings. I love you more than words can express. May God continue to richly bless and keep you is my prayer.

Acknowledgements

First and foremost, I give honor to my LORD and Savior Jesus Christ who is the head of my life. God has been good to me and He has equipped and blessed me with the talent and ability to write this book. I say "thank You Lord" because I realize that I can do nothing without God but with Him all things are possible. So, I give God all the praise, glory, and honor that He so rightfully deserves. I love the Lord because He first loved me!

A special thank you to Dr. C Dexter Wise III, and Dr. Shirley D. Wise, Pastor and Co-Pastor of Faith Ministries Church and President of the Wise School of Ministry, Columbus, Ohio. Dr. Wise, you consistently challenged me to step outside of my comfort zone and to pursue my dreams. You inspired, encouraged, and supported me during my studies at The Wise School of Ministry and as a leader at Faith Ministries Church, for that, I say thank you and may God continue to richly bless you!

To the State of Florida Full Gospel Baptist Church Fellowship West District Overseer and Pastor of Friendship Missionary Baptist Church, Pensacola, Florida, Pastor LuTimothy May, Sr., Thank you for your kind words of encouragement, your outstanding leadership, love, and support. May God continue to smile on you and bless you.

To Pastor Charles Thomas and St. James Missionary Baptist Church, Pensacola, Florida. Thank you for your love and support toward me. May God continue to richly bless you.

To my beloved mother Helen Madison, thank you for being my mother, my number one supporter, and my best friend. You are an exceptional role model and a genuine women of God. Thank you for loving, supporting and caring for us when no one else was concerned. You taught us the value of hard work, dedication and perseverance. You said that we could achieve anything in life if we put our trust in God. Most importantly, you taught us to love the Lord with all of our heart, mind, spirit, body, and soul. Thank you for your unconditional love. I love you greatly. May God continue to richly bless you is my prayer.

To my amazing sister Linda Burnett, niece Lyndrika Burnett, nephews: Marcus Clark, Martego Clark, and Tyjaun Madison, my great nephew Kamari Everheart, my great niece Kamora Flowers, my aunt Rosie Ptomy, cousins Willie Mae Ross, Connie Fails, Tamesha Austin-Hall, and my special friends: Samuel Andrews Jr, Duke A. Evans, Lashanda Jackson, Donna Chatman, Katrina Huff-Williams, Lachell Sullivan-Dexter, Barbara Harris, Linda Boston, Sheila Welch, Barbara and Dec. Frank Cleveland, Doris White, Rev. Lillie and Rev. Jacob King, Cheryl and Rev. Robbie Robinson, Jr., Sharon Williams, Minister Ramona Stromas, Minister Karen Johnson, and Evangelist Sandra Banks, thank you all for the love and support that you have shown me throughout the years.

A special thank you to Mrs. Rosetta Jamieson-Thomas for the consultation and for encouraging me to self-publish this book. Thank you to my editor Kara Luckett, stylist Dawnisa Straughter, photographer Simone Owens, assistant Kamora Flowers and graphic design by Pixel Studios, Bosnia and Herzegovina. Finally, I would like to express my sincere thank you and appreciation to each of you my valued readers. May God continue to immensely bless each of you is my prayer.

Preface

It is my sincere hope and prayer that everyone that reads this book will be encouraged, inspired, and better equipped to face the obstacles and adversities by conquering with Christ and overcoming your adversities through the Word of God. *Nay, in all these things we are more than conquerors through him that loved us. Romans 8:37. For we wrestle not against flesh and blood but against principalities, against powers, against the rulers of the darkness of this world, against spiritual wickedness in high places. Ephesians 6:12.* Though, we wrestle, we do not wrestle alone, God is with us. God has sent His Word to heal us. And, we are, indeed, healed, saved, delivered and set free by the blood of the Lamb and the word of our testimony. Rev. 12:11. I challenge each of you to rise above your circumstances. Move beyond your comfort zone and trust God to do what no one else can do in your life. God cares for you and He loves you exceedingly!

Chapter One
Overcoming Addictions

A Prayer for Overcoming Addictions

Dear Heavenly Father, I come before You today on behalf of all the men, women, boys and girls that are battling addictions of any kind. We bind every demonic spirit and every strong hold of the enemy. We come against drug, alcohol, pornography, sex, lying, cheating and stealing addictions. We take power and authority over principalities, rulers of darkness and spiritual wickedness in high places. I pray that Your Holy Spirit will overflow in the lives of your people. Give them grace, give them power and give them strength as they learn to trust and believe in You for deliverance. It is in Jesus name we pray. Amen

---

Key Scripture: And do not get drunk with wine, for that is sin but be filled with the Spirit, addressing one another in psalms and hymns and spiritual songs. Ephesians 5:18

Objective: After reading this chapter the reader should be able to discuss the meaning of addiction. Discuss practical reasons why people become addicted, common forms of addiction, how to overcome addiction, how to get help for addiction, and biblical references relating to addiction.

What is Addiction?

Addiction is a dependency on or an over-indulgence in something or someone in order to satisfy a need or a craving. In fact, addiction is a serious mental illness in which victims are often in denial resulting in delayed to little or no professional treatment at all. Studies have proven that there are numerous reasons why people become addicted. Most notably, people become addicted as a result of a life changing catastrophe (i.e., divorce, rejection, low self-esteem, dependency on prescription medications, grief, depression, loneliness, disappointments, failures, anger, self-guilt, and a loss of job) just to name a few.

Consequently, Addiction does not discriminate based on age, race, color, creed, ethnicity, sexual orientation, religious affiliations, gender or education. Studies have shown that many people refuse treatment, mainly due to denial, but regardless to the rationale, *there is a cure for addiction.*

Below is a list of some recognizable signs of addiction

1. A willingness to do anything, including but not limited to, breaking the law in order to get money to buy drugs
2. Stealing and committing crimes
3. Prostitution
4. Lying and cheating
5. Withdrawal symptoms
6. Irritability

Five warning signs specific to Video games and Internet addiction:

1. Disrupted regular life pattern. If a person plays games all night long and sleeps in the daytime.
2. If the person loses his or her job, or stops going to school in order to be online or to play a game.
3. Does the person have to play for extended periods in order to get the same level of enjoyment from the game?
4. Does the person appear to be withdrawal when they are not engaged in the game or on the internet?
5. Does the person experience cravings for the game when they are not on line or playing?

What are some Forms of Addiction?

Drugs
Alcohol
Pornography
Sex
Lying
Cheating
Stealing
Overeating
Video games
Gambling
Prostitution

How to Overcome Addiction

- ✓ Praying to God and asking him to help you overcome your addiction.
- ✓ Seek Counseling from a spiritual and professional advisor
- ✓ Request prescription medication
- ✓ Participate in a treatment program
- ✓ Healthy eating habits, proper sleep, and exercise
- ✓ Participation in a 12-step recovery program

What does the Bible say about Addiction?

For freedom Christ has set us free; stand firm therefore, and do not submit again to a yoke of bondage. Galatians 5:1
Therefore, if anyone is in Christ, he is a new creation. The old has passed away; behold, the news has come. 2 Corinthians 5:17
Do you not know that if you present yourselves to anyone as obedient slaves, you are slaves of the one whom you obey, either of sin, which leads to death, or of obedience which leads to righteousness? Romans 6:16
Do not be deceived: Bad company ruins good morals. 1 Corinthians 15:33
No temptation has overtaken you that are not common to man. God is faithful and he will not let you be tempted beyond your ability, but with the temptation he will also provide the way of escape, that you may be able to endure it. 1 Corinthians 10:13
Submit yourselves therefore to God. Resist the devil and he will flee from you. James 4:7
If the Son therefore shall make you free, ye shall be free indeed. 1 John 8:36

Helpful Resources Regarding Addiction?

Drug, Alcohol, Sex, Pornography, Gambling, Eating disorders, Tobacco, Prostitution. 1-800-943-0566. www.addictions.com

Knowledge Check

Please mark your answers to the following questions (T) true or (F) false.

1. T/F   Addiction is a dependency on or an over indulgences in something or someone in order to satisfy a need or a craving.

2. T/F   Willingness to do anything, including but not limited to breaking the law to get money to buy drugs is a sign of addiction

3. T/F   There is no cure for addiction

Chapter Two
Overcoming Depression

A Prayer for those Suffering from Depression

Father God, in the mighty name of Jesus, I come before You today lifting up every man, woman, boy, and girl that is battling depression. I pray Father that You will lift them up on every leaning side and that You will send Your Holy Spirit to minister to their hearts. Father, I pray that you will send Your anointing because the anointing will break every yoke and destroy every stronghold. For You are God and besides You there is no other. Lord God show Yourself mighty as You have done so many times before. What the enemy meant for bad, allow it to be turned around for their good. Work all things out for the good of those that love the Lord and called according to His purpose. Romans 8:28. Thank You Lord that You have given them power and authority to speak to depression and today we command depression to leave Your people and to set them free in the name of Jesus. For those that the Son sets free are free, indeed. Father, we give You all the praise, glory and honor for what You have done, for what You are doing and for what You will do in the lives of Your people. In Jesus name we pray. Amen.

Key Scripture: When the righteous cry for help, the LORD hears and delivers them out of all their troubles. Psalms 34:17

Objective: After reading this chapter, the reader should be able to discuss the meaning of depression, identify some common reasons why people suffer from depression, biblical references relating to depression, common signs and symptoms of depression, counseling strategies for depression and how to get help for depression.

Nay, in all these things we are more than conquerors through Him that love us. Romans 8:37

Depression is a common and serious medical mood disorder that adversely affects how you feel, the way you think, and how you act. Depression results in feelings of sadness and loss of interest in everyday activities. Depression can lead to emotional and physical problems. Depression affects more than 45 million Americans every year and is the leading cause of disability in the U.S. for people between the ages of 15 to 45 years. Women outnumber men in that one out of every four women suffer from signs of depression whereas only one out of every eight men experience signs of depression according to the National Institute of Health.

Common truths about depression

- Depression is a medical illness
- Depression is a mental illness
- Depression stems from an inability to love yourself
- Depression is an offset of low self-esteem
- Depression oppresses your spirit
- Depression stems from unresolved or suppressed bitterness, anger, hatred, hurt, hopelessness, guilt, shame, loss or grieving, and rejection.
- Depression persists and intensifies due to a lack of spiritual connection and biblical foundation
- Depression is caused by unconfessed sin
- Depression results from fears

Symptoms of Depression

Physical Symptoms	Emotional Symptoms	Behavioral Symptoms
Dry mouth	Anxiety	Crying
Excessive perspiration	Depression	Disrupted eating habits
Frequent illnesses	Fatigue	Disrupted sleeping habits
Gastrointestinal problems	Hypervigilance	Harsh treatment of others
Grinding of teeth	Impulsiveness	Problems communicating
Headaches	Inability to concentrate	Sexual problems
High blood pressure	Irritability	Social isolation
Pounding heart	Trouble remembering things	Increased use of alcohol or drugs
Stiff neck or back pain	Edginess	Increased use of alcohol or drugs

Anxiety in the heart of man causes depression, but a good word makes it glad Proverbs 12:25 (NKJV). God provides both a diagnosis and prescription that can help individuals to cope with depression. Replace anxiety in your heart with a word from God.

Jesus is the answer in conquering Depression

"Come unto me, all ye that labour and are heavy laden, and I will give you rest. Take my yoke upon you, and learn of me; for I am meek and lowly in heart: and ye shall find rest unto your souls." Matthew 11:28-29

Faith, Hope and Love

Conquering depression through Faith

Now faith is the substance of things hoped for and the evidence of things not seem. Hebrews 11:1

Exercising your faith in a higher power will help you in overcoming depression. If you believe and have faith that God can do anything, then half the battle has already been won and you're well on your way to conquering your depression through Christ! An important question to consider is "Do you have mustard seed faith?" "Do you have enough faith to move a mountain?" God specializes in things that seem impossible. While battling depression may seem impossible to overcome or perhaps, too difficult to overcome, you can conquer depression through your faith in God. If you are experiencing feelings of anxiety, excitement or thoughts of giving up, may I submit to you a cure? *Jesus is the cure. Jesus is the answer.* I encourage you to hang in there, don't give up and don't give in. Your blessing is on the way. Don't be dismayed. You are not in despair. You are not a failure, **you are a winner and you are a conqueror through Christ!** There is hope for you. Your hope is in Jesus, the Son of the living God. Have faith in God and know that *you can do all things through Christ that strengthens you. Philippians 4:13*

Conquering depression through Hope

Now the God of hope fill you with all joy and peace in believing, that ye may abound in hope, through the power of the Holy Ghost.
Romans 15:13

God is our eternal hope. He is a present help in the time of need. God's hope allows you to experience joy and peace through the power of the Holy Spirit. Therefore, I encourage you to build your hope on eternal things, build your hope on Godly things and finally, build your hope on nothing less than the blood of Jesus and His righteousness. *Through the encouragement of the Scriptures, we might have hope. Romans 15:4.* **Stop allowing your past mistakes to determine your future.** Your later days will be greater than your former. Rest assured that God knows the plans and thoughts that He has for you; thoughts of peace and not evil, thoughts of prosperity and not harm but to give you an expected end and abundant life. Jeremiah 29:11. **Did you know that God is bigger than any mistake that you may have made in life?** Yes, the LORD is BIGGER and the LORD is BETTER and *"The Grace of God in Jesus is the Sum of all Hope." Colossians 1:5; 1 Timothy 1:1*

Conquering depression through Love

Above all, love each other deeply, because love covers a multitude of sins. 1 Peter 4:8

If you love God, yourself, and others without limitations, judgement, or fear then you will experience the highest degree of love, Agape love. Agape love is loving in spite of shortcomings and learning to accept yourself and others just as you are. With that being said, you have now overcome one of life's greatest fear and achieved the best gift of all. While many people are afraid to love due to past hurts, failures and/or fear of rejection, some people have mastered the trade and have obtained the key to unlocking depression. Equally important is the ability to forgive others as you will have them to forgive you. Learn to *live, love, and laugh often.* Perhaps, you are aware of someone that may be going through a difficult time in life. What can you do to make a difference? Why not consider sending a card, an encouraging message, a phone call, or simply saying a prayer? You will be amazingly surprised of the positive difference that your act of kindness generates. Remember, when you bless others, God will bless you in return. Moreover, we are commanded to love one another because God is love; and every one that loveth is born of God, and knoweth God. For God so loved the world that He gave His only begotten Son, that whosoever believeth in Him should not perish, but have everlasting life. John 3:16

Practical Strategies for Coping with Depression

1. Identify the causes of your depression
2. Consult with a licensed Psychiatrist
3. Take Antidepressant Medication
4. Exercise and healthy eating
5. Communicate your feelings with family or friends
6. Shift your perspective and interpretation of the way you think and feel about situations to positive thoughts.
7. Support groups/enrollment in an impatient treatment center
8. Pray and Listen to motivational & inspirational messages
9. Attend a local Bible Based Church
10. Seek Counseling

What does the Bible say about Depression?

In a desert land he found him, in a barren and howling waste. He shielded him and cared for him; he guarded him as the apple of his eye. Deuteronomy 32:10
But you, O LORD, are a shield about me, my glory, and the lifter of my head. Psalms 3:3
It is the LORD who goes before you. He will be with you; he will not leave you or forsake you. Do not fear or be dismayed. Deuteronomy 31:8
When the righteous cry for help, the LORD hears and delivers them out of all their troubles. Psalms 34:17
Many are the sorrows of the wicked, but steadfast love surrounds the one who trusts in the LORD. Psalms 32:10
I waited patiently for the LORD; he inclined to me and heard my cry. He drew me up from the pit of destruction, out of the miry bog, and set my feet upon a rock, making my steps secure. He put a new song in my mouth, a song of praise to our God. Many will see and fear, and put their trust in the LORD. Psalms 40:1-3
Why are you cast down, O my soul, and why are you in turmoil within me? Hope in God; for I shall again praise him, my salvation and my God. Psalms 42:11
Humble yourselves therefore under the mighty hand of God, that he may exalt you in due time: Casting all your care upon him; for He careth for you. 1 Peter 5:6-7
Trust in the LORD, and do good; dwell in the land and befriend faithfulness. Delight yourself in the LORD, and he will give you the desires of your heart. Psalms 37:3-4
For I know the plans I have for you, declares the LORD, plans for welfare and not for evil, to give you a future and a hope. Jeremiah 29:11
I have said these things to you, that in me you may have peace. In the world you will have tribulation. But take heart; I have overcome the world. John 16:33

Knowledge Check

Please mark your answers to the following questions (T) true or (F) false.

1. T/F   Depression is a mental and a medical illness that adversely affects the way you feel, think and act.

2. T/F   Depression affects more than 15 million Americans every year and is the leading cause of disability in the U.S. for people between the ages of 15 to 45 years.

3. T/F   According to the National Institute of Health men are more likely to suffer from signs of depression than women.

Helpful Resources for Depression
Psych Central   www.psychcentral.com
NeuroStar R TMS Therapy www.neurostar.com/Depression/Treatement
Veterans with Depression www.maketheconnection.net/Depression
Online Depression Video Course www.Alta-wellness.thinkific.com
Coping with Depression www.helpguide.org
THIS WAY UP www.thiswayup.com
Self-help Depression and Anxiety www.depression.org.nz
Sage Neuroscience www.sageclinic.org/tms or (505) 884-1114
Free Mental Health Assistance for Depression www.mentalhealthline.org
Brehm.org www.brehm.org/ or (618) 457-0371
Depression/NAMI: National Alliance on Mental Illness www.nami.org
Health Line www.healthfinder.gov
Counseling 4 Christians www.counseling4christians.com (407) 322-6868

Seek Counseling for Depression

Listen to counsel and accept discipline. The counsel of the Lord, it will stand. Proverbs 19:20

What is counseling?
Counseling is the act of providing advice, support and guidance in dealing with and resolving personal and emotional problems. Counseling deals with personal, social, vocational empowerment and education concerns. The areas may include intra and interpersonal concerns related to mental health, marriage, divorce, depression, suicidal thoughts, addiction, and family issues just to name a few. Counseling is a theory-based process in which clients learn how to make decisions and formulate new ways of behaving, feeling and thinking. Successful outcomes require setting obtainable goals. Counseling involves both choice and change, evolving through distinct stages such as exploration, goal setting and action.

Apparently, Jesus knew that his departure was drawing near and that He would soon have to return unto his Father's house. Jesus knew how ill prepared and misguided we would be here on Earth after His departure. Consequently, He sent the Holy Spirit to dwell with us. "I will ask the Father, and He will give you another Helper (Counselor) John 14:16. The Holy Spirit is the third person of the God head. The Holy Spirit is our comforter. He is our guide, and our ultimate counselor. He leads and guides us into all righteousness. *God for us, Jesus in us, and the Holy Spirit with us.*

Common reasons to seek counseling

Depression
Mental Illness
Marital Issues
Addictions
Suicidal thoughts
Divorce
Marriage
Relationship Issues
Life Altering Decisions/Crises
Grief and coping with the loss of a loved one
Domestic Violence
Anger Management
Financial Management

Biblical Truths Regarding Counseling

A wise man is he who listens to counsel. Proverbs 12:15
Listen to counsel and accept discipline. The counsel of the Lord, it will stand. Proverbs 19:20
His name will be called wonderful Counselor, The mighty God, The everlasting Father, and The Prince of Peace. Isaiah 9:6
The Helper, I will send Him to you. John 16:7
The Helper, the Holy Spirit will teach you all things. John 14:26

Chapter Three
Managing Anger

A Prayer for Anger

Father God in the name of Jesus I come before You today to give you praise, glory and honor. Thank you for Your abundance of good, and that You are good all the time. I come to You on behalf of those that are experiencing anger issues. I pray that You will intervene in their lives and exchange anger with Your love, peace, and joy. Help them to effectively manage and control anger with wisdom and knowledge. Teach them how to walk in calmness. May Your Holy Spirit dwell with them forever. We seal it and we count it as done in Jesus name we pray. Amen.

Key Scripture: He that is slow to anger is better than the mighty; and he that ruleth his spirit than he that taketh a city. Proverbs 16:32

Objective: After reading this chapter on managing anger you should be able to identify the meaning of anger, recognize the signs and triggers, discover practical ways to manage anger, discover what the bible says regarding anger and identify helpful resources.

Managing Anger

What is Anger?

Anger is a strong feeling of displeasure or hostility. It is a normal emotion with a wide range of intensity from mild irritation and frustration to rage. It is a signal that we think we are being treated unfairly. It is noteworthy to mention that not all anger is bad. Some anger may be good, however, you must learn to control anger before it controls you. Have you ever wondered why people get so angry over small things or perhaps, they get angry for no apparent reason at all? Unfortunately, many people may suffer from an undiagnosed medical condition and may experience difficulties in controlling and identifying a valid reason for their angry. While we are aware that some people get angry because things don't always go their way or they feel that they are losing control, there are individuals that have valid reasons for getting angry. As we search the scriptures regarding this issue of anger, we are instructed in *Ephesians 4:26 to "Be ye angry, and sin not."* As such, we understand that the primary issue is not in the anger, but rather, in the sin as a result of anger.

So, when you hear the word angry, is there a particular person that comes to your mind? If you answered yes, then you are in the majority. Frankly, when most people hear the word angry they immediately think of someone in their inner circle (i.e. a mother or father, a sibling, a child (ren), or a close friend.) Regardless to who comes to mind when you hear the word angry, you must take immediate steps to help that individual identify the triggers and determine alternative ways to resolve the anger. *While anger is twofold and occurs as a result of emotional hurt coupled with suppressed feelings of disappointment and/or fear of something horrible that may have occurred, it is a proven fact that unresolved anger is evident in one's behavior and actions.* It is imperative to get to the root cause of the anger and if necessary seek professional help.

---If life gives you Lemons, make lemonade---
Dale Carnegie

Practical Keys to Managing Anger

- Attitude – How do you feel?
    - Admit that you have an anger problem
    - Determine the best course of action
    - Create a plan for managing anger
    - Monitor your progress daily
    - Examine and document your results

- Behavior – How do you react?
    - Take appropriate steps to change your behavior
    - Discover positive ways to turn negative energy into something good
    - Engage in positive behavior change
    - Acknowledge your accomplishments

- Mindset – What do you think?
    - Pray and ask God to help you to control your anger
    - Change the way you think about the situation
    - Determine to think positive thoughts
    - Surround yourself with positive people
    - Read inspirational devotions or the Bible

Life is less about what happens to you and more about how you respond to what happens to you in life.

Getting to the Root Cause of Anger

Ephesians 4:26. Be ye angry and sin not

Getting to the root cause of anger involves recognizing the signs and identifying the cause. Can you recall a time that you may have gotten upset or angry with someone because they did not speak to you? Sounds trivial, right? Absolutely, but surprisingly many people get upset over trivial things and if the truth be told, we are all guilty of this type of behavior primarily due to perception. Hence, we perceived a certain thing or situation to be bigger than what it really was. We allow our emotions to take over and we perceive that we are being excluded, overlooked, discredited, or disrespected. These are just a few examples of incidents that can lead to valid feelings of anger. *Remember that getting angry is not wrong. The problem exist when you allow anger to control you.*

Seven keys to coping with anger:

1. Pray to God for help
2. Exercise (walk or run)
3. Talk about your feelings of anger to a friend or someone you trust.
4. Redirect your anger to something positive
5. Count to 10 and take a deep breath
6. Write about what you are feeling
7. Take a step back and deal with it when you have calmed down.

Pray that God will help you and give you peace. Submit all of your cares and worries to God because He cares for you. Forgive others as God has forgiven you and accept the things that you cannot change and pray for wisdom to know the difference.

Helpful Resources

Restore Counseling   614-721-8235
www.restorecounsel.com

Native Remedies   1-800-683-1235
www.nativeremedies.com

American Psychological Association   1-800-374-2721
www.apa.org

APA   202-336-5500
www.apa.org

Life Script
www.lifescript.com

Ask.com
www.ask.com/helpwithangerissues

Directions Counseling Group   614-888-9200
www.directionscounseling.com

What does the Bible says about Anger?

The LORD is gracious and full of compassion; slow to anger and of great mercy. Psalms 145:8
A God ready to pardon, gracious and merciful, slow to anger and of great kindness. Nehemiah 9:17
For his anger endureth but a moment; In his favour is life: weeping may endure for a night, but joy cometh in the morning. Psalms 30:5
Wherefore, my beloved brethren, let every man be swift to hear, slow to speak, slow to wrath: For the wrath of man worketh not the righteousness of God. James 1:19-20
Be not hasty in the spirit to be angry: for anger resteth in the bosom of fools. Ecclesiastes 7:9
He that is soon angry dealeth foolishly. Proverbs 14;17
He that is slow to anger is better than the mighty; and he that ruleth his spirit than he that taketh a city. Proverbs 16:32
A wrathful man stirreth up strife: but he that is slow to anger appeaseth strife. Proverbs 15:18.
An angry man stirred up strife, and a furious man abounded in transgression. Proverbs 29:22
Cease from anger and forsake wrath: fret not thyself in any wise to do evil. Psalms 37:8

Make no friendship with an angry man; and with a furious man thou shalt not go: Lest thou learn his ways, and get a snare to thy soul. Proverbs 22:24
A soft answer turneth away wrath: but grievous words stir up anger. Proverbs 15:1
Father, provoke not your children to anger, lest they be discouraged. Colossians 3:21
Be ye angry, and sin not; let not the sun go down upon your wrath: Ephesians 4:26
The discretion of a man deferreth his anger; and it is his glory to pass over a transgression. Proverbs 19:11
It is better to dwell in the wilderness, than with a contentious and an angry women. Proverbs 21:19
But I say unto you, that whosoever is angry with his brother without a cause shall be I danger of the judgment. Matthew 5:22

Knowledge Check

Please mark your answers to the following questions (T) true or (F) false.

1. T/F   Anger is twofold and occurs as a result of emotional hurt coupled with suppressed feelings of disappointment and/or fear of something horrible that may have occurred

2. T/F Anger is a strong feeling of displeasure or hostility. It is a normal emotion with a wide range of intensity from mild irritation and frustration to rage. .

3. T/F   Getting to the root cause of anger involves recognizing the signs and identifying the cause

Chapter Four
Suicide Prevention

A Prayer for Those Suffering with Suicidal Thoughts

Father God, in the name of Jesus, I come before You today on behalf of those suffering with suicidal thoughts. Father, I pray that You will deliver them and give them peace. Give them a peace that will surpass all understanding. I pray that You will protect them from the enemy of suicide. Destroy every strong hold of the enemy and break every yoke of bondage. I come against and tear down strong holds, principalities, and spiritual wickedness in high places. I come against the spirit of fear, depression and suicidal thoughts. I come against the spirit of bi-polar and schizophrenia disorders. I come against mental disorders and every sickness of the mind. I command every demonic spirit to flee and leave God's people. Devil return to the pits of hell from whence thy cometh. Get thee behind us Satan. I come against the spirit of darkness and destruction. Holy Spirit have Your way in this place. Spirit of the living God rule and abide forever. Father, show Yourself strong and mighty. Send Your love and power. You are Jehovah Jireh, You are the Lord our provider and there is nothing too hard for You. Thank you for dispatching ministering Angels on our behalf. Thank you for hearing and answering our prayers, but most of all, thank you that the battle has already been won over 2000 years ago on Calvary. You are our joy, You are our peace, You are our hope for tomorrow in Jesus name we pray. Amen.

Key Scripture: He heals the brokenhearted and bins up their wounds. Psalms 147:3

Objective: After reading this chapter on suicide prevention you should be able to identify the meaning and warning signs of suicide, identify suicide contributors, identify helpful resources and discover what the bible has to say regarding suicide.

> *When everything seems to be going against you,*
> *Remember that the airplane takes off*
> *Against the wind,*
> *Not with it.*
> *Henry Ford, Author*

Suicide Prevention

What is Suicide?

Suicide is the act of intentionally causing one's own death. Suicide is a way for people to escape from emotional pain or suffering. The suicide rate is higher among white men between the ages of 15 and 29. It's the second most common cause of death in adolescence. Some risk factors include, but are not limited to mental disorders such as depression, bipolar disorder, schizophrenia personality disorders and substance abuse such as alcoholism and benzodiazepines. Suicide is a chronic treatable illness. Mental health problems do not discriminate among gender, race, age, ethnicity, or origin.

An estimated 40% of Medicaid recipients under the Affordable Care Act have mental health issues. Insurance coverage for these individuals are primarily nonexistent. Consequently, mental health care coverage for the under privilege is extremely difficult.

Suicidal Facts

Due to social stigmatization, people whose gender identity does not align with their assigned sex are at high risk of suicide. Specifically, transgender, lesbian, gay, and bisexual people. The World Suicide Prevention Day is observed annually on September 10.

What's the Truth Regarding Suicidal Thoughts?

The truth is that your life matters. Your very existence matters to God and it matters to the people around you. God has a purpose and a plan for your life. You are valued, you are loved, and you are a gift from God. *God's Grace Saved You*! His Grace is sufficient for you. God's mercies toward you are new everyday so begin to focus less on your little problem(s) and more on your Great Big God. God is bigger than any situation or problem that you may be experiencing. God is bigger than depression, addiction, failures, disappointments, loneliness, drugs, alcohol, and sex addictions. He's bigger than the things that seemingly tears you apart. Don't give up on God because He will not give up on you. The absolute truth about the matter is that God loves you unconditionally and you, likewise, must learn to love yourself because the greatest gift of all is to love yourself. Remember to always *Live, Love and Laugh often!*

What are the 10 Warning Signs of Suicide?

If you or someone that you know are experiencing the following warning signs you should contact ***the National Suicide Prevention Hotline at 1-800-273-8255:***

1. Suicidal conversation – talking about dying or self-harm or statements such as "I wish I were dead."
2. Obsession with guns, knives or taking pills.
3. Posting comments about dying on Facebook or other social media
4. Feelings of hopelessness and helplessness.
5. Feeling worthlessness, guilt, shame, and self-hatred.
6. Creating a will and giving away possessions
7. Unusual visits to say goodbye
8. Isolation from family and friends
9. Substance abuse
10. A sudden calmness and peace after extreme depression.

Suicidal Contributors

<u>Health</u>

Major change in eating habits

Major change in sleeping habits

<u>Work</u>

Change in a new type of work

Increase or decrease in your responsibilities at work

Demotion, transfer, grievance, discrimination

Major Employment Change

Retirement, loss of job, laid off or fired

<u>Home and Family</u>

Major change in living conditions

Change in residence

Out of State move

Divorce

Separation

Miscarriage or abortion

Death of a family member

Personal and Social Change

Change in school or college

Change in religious beliefs

Suicidal Contributors Continue

Change in a close personal relationship
Violation of the law
Incarceration
<u>Finance</u>
Decrease in income
Credit difficulties
Foreclosures
Repossessions
IRS indebtedness
Loss or damage to personal property

Suicide Statistics

Based on a New York Times 2016 report regarding Suicide Rate in the U.S., the suicide rate in the U.S. surged to a 30-year high. The rate was substantial among middle aged men and women in America. The rate for middle-aged women, ages 45 to 64 jumped by 63% and rose by 43% for men in the same age range. The overall suicide rate rose by 24% from 1999 to 2014, according to the National Center for Health Statistics. The nation's overall suicide rate increased to 13 per 100,000 people; the highest since 1986. A total of 42,773 people died from suicide in 2014 compared with 29,199 in 1999. In 2016, there were 44,965 recorded suicides up from 42,773 in 2014. In 2015, suicide was the seventh leading cause of death for males and the 14th leading cause of death for females. Additionally, it was the second leading cause of death for young people age 15 to 24 and the third leading cause of death for those between the ages of 10 and 14 from 1999 to 2010. The rate for ages 35 to 64 increased nearly 30%. The largest increase were among men in their fifties.

In a 2014 study conducted by the American Foundation for Suicide Prevention discovered the following:

1. The annual age-adjusted suicide rate is 13.26 per 100,000 individuals.
2. Men die from suicide 3.5 times more often than women
3. Women attempt suicide 2 times more often than men
4. On average, there are 121 suicides per day
5. White males accounted for 7 of 10 suicides in 2015
6. A firearm is used in almost 50% of all suicides
7. The rate of suicide is highest in middle age- white men

How do I overcome suicidal thoughts?

Preventive methods include but not limited to:

- Cognitive behavioral therapy
- Crisis hotlines
- Economic development
- Psychometric evaluation using the Beck Depression Inventory or the Geriatric Depression Scale
- Suicide prevention contracts agreeing to not harm yourself
- Dialectical behavior therapy (adolescents)
- Antidepressants (controversial)
- Lithium
- Clozapine

National Suicide Prevention Lifeline

The National Suicide Prevention Lifeline (1-800-273-TALK (8255) is a U.S. based suicide prevention network of 161 crisis centers that provides 24/7 toll-free hotline assistance to anyone in emotional distress. After dialing 1-800-273-8255, the caller is routed to their nearest crisis center to receive immediate counseling and local mental health referrals. Contact via web address: www.suicidepreventionlifeline.org.

Jehovah Rapha "The Lord Heals" from all Sicknesses and Diseases"

By His stripes we have been healed. The Bible clearly declares that Jesus died on the Cross for the sins of the world. According to Matthew 8:17 he took our infirmities and bore our sicknesses. Therefore, healing and deliverance belong to you. Jesus purchased it by his redemptive blood.

Psalms 107:20 tells us that God sent His word and healed them and delivered them from their destructions.

Psalms 103:3 Who forgiveth all thine iniquities; who healeth all thy diseases.

1 Peter 2:24 Who his own self bare our sins in his own body on the Cross that we, being dead to sins, should live unto righteousness: by whose stripes ye were healed.

Matthew 8:16 When evening had come, they brought to Him many who were demon-possessed. And He cast out the spirits with a word, and healed all who were sick, that it might be fulfilled which was spoken by Isaiah the prophet, saying "He Himself took our infirmities and bore our sicknesses."

Exodus 15:26 If thou will diligently hearken to the voice of the LORD thy God, and wilt do that which is right in his sight, and wilt give ear to his commandments and keep all his statutes, I will put none of these diseases upon thee which I have brought upon the Egyptians; for I am the LORD that healeth thee.

What does the Bible say about Suicide?

Humble yourselves, therefore, under God's mighty hand, that he may lift you up in due time. Cast all your anxiety on him because he cares for you. 1 Peter 5:6-7
Then Jesus told his disciples a parable to show them that they should always pray and not give up. Luke 18:1
Therefore, the redeemed of the Lord shall return, and come with singing unto Zion; and everlasting joy shall be upon their head: they shall obtain gladness and joy; and sorrow and mourning shall flee away. Isaiah 51:11
Though I walk in the midst of trouble, thou will revive me: thou shall stretch forth thine hand against the wrath of mine enemies, and thy right hand shall save me. Psalms: 138:7
We are troubled on every side, yet not distressed; we are perplexed, but not in despair; persecuted but not forsaken; cast down, but not destroyed. 2 Corinthians 4:8-9
Being confident of this very thing, that he who hath begun a good work in you will perform it until the day of Jesus Christ. Philippians 1:6
And let us not be weary in well doing: for in due season we shall reap if we faint not. Galatians 6:9
Nothing will be able to separate us from the love of God that is in Christ Jesus our Lord. Romans 8:39

Knowledge Check

Please mark your answers to the following questions (T) true or (F) false.

1. T/F   Due to social stigmatization, people whose gender identity does not align with their assigned sex are at high risk of suicide.

2. T/F   The suicide rate is higher among women between the ages of 15 and 26. It's the number one most common cause of death in adolescence.

3. T/F   Mental health problems do not discriminate among gender, race, age, ethnicity, or origin. An estimated 40% of Medicaid recipients under the Affordable Care Act have mental health issues.

Helpful Resources

Crisis Hotline   877-435-2621
www.mentalhealthline.org

National Suicide Prevention Lifeline   1-800-273-8255
www.suicidepreventionLifeline.org

Chapter Five
Domestic Violence & Rape

A Prayer for Victims of Domestic Violence

Father Jehovah, in the name of Jesus I come boldly before the throne of Grace. I come giving You praise, glory and honor. I come pleading the blood of Jesus on behalf of the people that are experiencing domestic violence. I pray that You will protect them, lead them, and guide them. Keep them safe from their perpetrator. Hide them in the secret place of Your tabernacle. Hide them under the shadow of Your wings. Keep them safe from all hurt, harm and danger. And I give You all the praise, glory, and honor, In Jesus name. Amen.

Key Scripture: My heart is in anguish within me, the terrors of death have fallen upon me. Fear and trembling come upon me, and horror overwhelms me. And I say "O that I had wings like a dove! I would fly away and be at rest. Yea, I would wander afar; I would lodge in the wilderness. I would haste to find me a shelter from the raging wind and tempest." Psalms 55:4-8.

Objective: After reading this chapter you should be able to explain the meaning of domestic violence, identify forms of abuse and behaviors of a perpetrator, identify warning signs and what to do if you or someone that you know is being abused, identify reasons why perpetrators abuse their victims, helpful resources for domestic violence, what the bible says about domestic violence.

What is Domestic Violence?
Domestic Violence is a pattern of repetitive, abusive behavior to maintain power and control over an intimate partner. Said behaviors are intended to physically harm, arouse fear, prevent a partner from doing what they wish, or force them to behave in ways they do not want.

Abuse includes the use of physical verbal, and/or sexual violence, threats, intimidation, emotional abuse, and economic deprivation. Many of these forms of abuse can be going on simultaneously.

Domestic Violence is a Chronic National Epidemic occurring behind closed doors. In 2012, over 665,000 women worldwide reported abuse. While abuse is widespread and claim the lives of thousands of women and men each year, over 70% of abuses are not persecuted and a substantial number of abuses go unreported mainly due to fear. In order to stop domestic violence, the victim has to want to get out of the abusive relationship.

You must love yourself more than you love the perpetrator. Possessive and controlling behaviors don't appear overnight neither do they end instantly but rather emerge and intensify as the relationship develops.

Forms of Abuse:

- *Emotional abuse* is the most common type of domestic violence

- *Physical abuse* involves slapping, beating, arm twisting, stabbing, strangling, burning, choking, kicking, threats with an object or weapon, murder, genital mutilation and others.

- *Verbal abuse* involves the use of derogatory words, criticism, belittling, and putting you down.

- *Sexual abuse* involves coerced sex, intimidation or physical force, forcing unwanted sexual acts or forcing sex with others.

- *Psychological abuse* involves intimidation, persecution, threats of abandonment or abuse, confinement to the home, surveillance, threats to take away custody of the children, destruction of objects, isolation, verbal aggression, and constant humiliation. Psychological abuse is the most common type of violence experienced by women and children.

- *Economic abuse* involves denial of funds, refusal to contribute financially, denial of food and basic needs and controlling access to health care, employment, etc.

In 2004, Congress passed the Anti-Violence Act against Women and Children. Children in the home also suffer from emotional and/or physical scars. These children are at high risk of becoming perpetrators.

In 2018 a trend involving the use of smart home technologies to harass and intimidate domestic violence victims emerged. Some of these digital devices include the following:

- Thermostat- Remotely changing the room temperature when away from the home.
- Lights- Remotely turning the lights on and off
- Doors- Remotely locking and unlocking the doors
- Smoke detectors- Controlling the device while away from home
- TV – Remotely changing the channels when away from home
- Appliances- manually resetting the devices while away

Warning Signs:
- Humiliation and ridicule in public
- Verbal Insults
- Physical Violence
- Controlling Behavior
- Unpredictable Mood Swings
- Picking at Faults
- Alienating your Family and Friends
- Blaming you for things that is not your fault
- Manipulation
- Calculated Outbursts

What to do if you or someone that you know is being abused

1. Contact the domestic violence abuse hotline
2. Help the abused person overcome "victim identity" by recognizing their inherent strengths, talents, skills, power and appreciation of self, and self-confidence
3. Convenience the person to locate to a safe environment
4. Report the abuse to your local authorities
5. Pray for that person's safety

Why do Perpetrators abuse their victims?

- Male chauvinistic mentality
- Drug and alcohol abuse
- Uncontrolled anger
- Low self-esteem
- Disappointments in self-achievements
- Jealousy
- Feelings of hurt
- Rejection
- Lack of self-control
- Diagnosed or undiagnosed mental illness
- Suffered abuse from others

Sexual Abuse

Know ye not that your body is the temple of the Holy Ghost [which is] in you, which ye have of God, and ye are not your own? 1 Corinthians 6:19

Sexual abuse or rape is any unwanted sexual contact without the consent of the victim. In short, rape is defined as an action to seize, take without permission, or carry off by force. *Leviticus 18:19-23 instructs us to refrain from approaching a woman to uncover her nakedness, as long as she is put apart for her uncleanness.* In this 18th chapter of Leviticus, Moses emphasizes the fact that it is not only unlawful to uncover or expose the nakedness of a woman but it is also sinful. The sin itself does not necessarily lie in the uncovering and nakedness of the victim, but rather in the sexual action that usually takes place when the woman is undressed. This unlawful act of sexual assault not only violates the woman's body but it also violates a covenant with Christ because we have learned from the scriptures that our bodies are the temple of the Holy Spirit. *Know ye not that the unrighteous shall not inherit the kingdom of God? Be not deceived: neither fornicators, nor idolaters, nor abusers of men, women or children. 1 Corinthians 6:9-11.*

Who are the offenders?

Sexual assault does not only happen to college students, women, and children but also men. Over 10% of all victims of rape are male. Every 2 minutes a sexual crime is committed in the U.S. Often, the perpetrator is a husband, boyfriend or former acquaintance, a family member or close friend. While some assaults are reported to the local authorities, there remain thousands of cases that go unreported each year. If you are a victim of sexual assault, contact your local authorities to report the incident.

Helpful Resources

Emergency 911
Rape Crisis Center 1-877-906-7273
www.recmsc.org/

National Sexual Assault Hotline 1-800-656-4673
https://rainn.org/statistics

National Network (RAINN) 1-800-656-4673. This organization will automatically connect you to your local U.S. Rape Crisis Center based on your area code

National Center for Victims of Crime 1-800-211-7996

The National Teen Dating Abuse Helpline
1-866-331-9474
www.thenationalteendating.org

ASHA-Ray of Hope   614-565-2918
www.asharayofhope.org

Choices, 24 hour crisis hotline   614-224-4663
www.choicesdvcols.org

Ohio Domestic Violence   1-800-934-9840
www.Ohiodomesticviolence.org

National Domestic Violence Hotline   1-800-799-7233
www.nationaldomesticviolence.org

Columbus Coalition Against Family Violence   614-722-5985
www.ccafv.org

Lighthouse- Mental Health   1-877-562-2565
www.lighthousenetwork.org

House of Ruth (DV)   1-877-988-5559

What does the Bible say about Domestic Violence and Rape?

You are valued in God's eyes; your whole body is regarded by God as a temple, a sacred place. Just as God does not want a temple defiled by violence, neither does God want you to be harmed. God's Spirit dwells in you and make you Holy. You deserve to live without fear or abuse. 1 Corinthians 6:19.
Husbands, love your wives and do not be harsh with them (Col 3:19). There are no excuses for violence and abusive behavior.
My heart is in anguish within me, the terrors of death have fallen upon me. Fear and trembling come upon me, and horror overwhelms me. And I say, "O that I had wings like a dove! I would fly away and be at rest. Yea, I would wander afar, I would lodge in the wilderness. I would haste to find me a shelter from the raging wind and tempest." Psalms 55:4-8.
Know ye not that the unrighteous shall not inherit the kingdom of God? Be not deceived: neither fornicators, nor idolaters, nor abusers of men, women or children. 1 Corinthians 6:9-11.
Now the works of the flesh are manifest, which are these; Adultery, fornication, uncleanness, lasciviousness. Galatians 5:19
The thief comes only to steal, kill and destroy; I come that you may have life and that more abundantly. John 10:10

Knowledge Check

Please mark your answers to the following questions (T) true or (F) false.

1. T/F   Domestic Violence is a pattern of repetitive abusive behavior to maintain power and control over an intimate partner and sexual assault does not only happen to college students, women, and children but also men.

2. T/F Abuse includes the use of physical verbal, sexual violence, threats, intimidation, emotional abuse and economic deprivation

3. T/F While some assaults are reported to the local authorities, there remain thousands of cases that go unreported each year

Chapter Six
Issues Impacting Women

A Prayer for Women

Father God, in the name of Jesus, I come before Your presence today to give You praise, glory and honor. Thank You for blessing women all over this world. Thank You for allowing women to accomplish their goals and to achieve major contributions in society. May Your divine love, grace, peace, and power continue to overflow and dwell in their lives. In Jesus name we pray. Amen.

Key Scripture: Charm is deceitful and beauty is vain, but a woman who fears the Lord is to be praised. Give her of the fruit of her hands, and let her works praise her in the gates. Proverbs 31:30-31 (ESV)

Objective: After reading this chapter regarding issues that impact women, you should be able to identify 12 personal keys to helpful living, identify the names of successful women and their accomplishments, identify a Proverbs 3:15 woman and discover what the Bible says about women.

Conquer with Christ   Marolyn Madison-Evans

The wisest of women builds her house, but folly with her own hands tears it down. Proverbs 14:1

Many people think that women in this country have achieved all their goals, however that could not be farther from the truth. While the effects of the Title VII have spilled over to every area of society and laws have changed women's rights in regards to abortion, divorce, child support, child custody, rape, employment as administrators and executives, much work has yet to be done. Accordingly, during the time of this research, the U.S. has yet to ratify the Equal Rights Amendment to our Constitution or The Convention on the Elimination of All Forms of Discrimination Against Women (CEDAW) Treaty, the International Bill of Rights for Women and is the only industrialized country that has not yet ratified CEDAW.

Women have made major accomplishments and contributions in helping to shape our nation's history and keep it strong through successful leadership and remarkable insight regarding political, social and economic development. For these reasons, it is in their honor that we celebrate National Women's History month in March. If we were to conduct a poll to observe some major accomplishments of successful women of today, prominent names such as Oprah Winfrey, Michelle Obama, Hillary Clinton, Serena and Venus Williams, Joyce, Myers, Rosa Parks, Sojourner Truth, Helen Steiner Rice, Meghan Markle, Robin Roberts, Cindy Trimm, Sarita Jakes would appear as most notable among the list. While these women have acquired major success and have achieved noteworthy contributions to society, it is the unspoken heroes and the countless women whose names we do not recognize that make women's history "Her" story. These are the courageous women who serve as doctors, lawyers, civil rights activists, astronauts, scientists, pilots, entrepreneurs, inventors, artists, writers, politicians, soldiers, teachers, mothers, and homemakers.

During a 2013 Women's History Month Program at the Defense Finance and Accounting Service in Columbus, Ohio, key note speaker Karlee Macer told those gathered that "women need to get beyond the toxic messages of body image and move toward roles that emphasize their capabilities." Women must not allow the media to define their worth; instead they must stress the importance of self-worth and confidence in who and what they are as women. ***Women must learn to accept and embrace their differences, body type and individuality.***

God has given women a uniqueness, great talents, knowledge and abilities. Women must remain committed to encouraging young girls and other women to be all that God has ordained them to be. Women must continue to demonstrate through hard work, education, perseverance and determination they can do and have anything they want in the world.

Likewise, society must refrain from sending the toxic message linking self-worth to body image. Women are distinctive, beautiful, and gifted individuals. Women were not designed to be duplicate copies, but rather one of a kind and irreplaceable. ***There are no carbon copies, imitations or counterfeits of you!***

Woman of God, do you know that you are more precious than rubies or gold? And all the things thou canst desire are not to be compared unto her. Proverbs 3:15

12 Personal keys to healthy living

1. Accept yourself –Embrace your talents, gifts, and uniqueness and love who you are.
2. Accept your body – You are shaped in God's image, you are an original, authentic and one of a kind.
3. Eat, sleep and exercise – Balance is the key to achieving success
4. Drink plenty of water – Water is an important necessity.
5. Reduce stress – Find time to relax and unwind
6. Say "No" – No is a complete sentence
7. Reduce stress at work– Find ways to decrease work related stress
8. Set goals – Set obtainable goals and achieve them
9. Balance responsibilities – Exercise, balance home life, parenting, career, and finance
10. Finance – Obtain financial stability
11. Spiritual–Seek God daily through prayer, meditation and devotion
12. Relationships – Foster loving, caring and positive relationships

Lord, we ain't what we want to be
We ain't what we ought to be
We aren't what we gonna be
But, thank God we ain't what we was
Author: Dr. Martin Luther King, Jr.

What does the Bible say about Women?

She is more precious than rubies; and all the things thou canst desire are not to be compared unto her. Proverbs 3:15
The wisest of women builds her house, but folly with her own hands tears it down. Proverbs 14:1
Charm is deceitful and beauty is vain but a woman who fears the Lord is to be praised. Give her of the fruit of her hands, and let her works praise her in the gates. Proverbs 31:30-31 (ESV)
There were also many women there, looking on from a distance, who had followed Jesus from Galilee, ministering to him. Matthew 27:55
The Lord God said, it is not good that the man should be alone; I will make him a helper fit for him. Genesis 2:18
A gracious woman gets honor and violent men gets riches. Proverbs 11:16
Older women likewise are to be reverent in behavior, not slanderers or slaves to much wine. They are to teach what is good and so train the young women to love their husbands and children, to be self-controlled, pure, working at home, kind and submissive to their own husbands that the word of God may not be reviled. Titus 2:3-5
He gives the barren woman a home, making her the joyous mother of children. Praise the LORD! Psalm 113:9

Knowledge Check

Please mark your answers to the following questions (T) true or (F) false.

1. T/F   The U.S. has yet to ratify the Equal Rights Amendment to our Constitution or the CEDAW Treaty, the International Bill of Rights for Women and is the only industrialized country that has not yet ratified CEDAW.

2. T/F   It is the spoken heroes and the countless women whose names we recognize that make women's history "Her" story.

3. T/F   Women have made major accomplishments and enormous contributions in helping to shape our nation's history and keep it strong through successful leadership and remarkable insight regarding political, social and economic development

Chapter Seven
Issues Impacting Men

A Prayer for Men

Father God, in the mighty, matchless and marvelous name of Jesus, I come before Your presence lifting up men all over the world. I pray that You will bless them, strengthen, and keep them. Help them to be great fathers and loving husbands. Help them to seek Your way, Your will, and Your wisdom for their lives. Teach them the art of loving God, themselves, their families and others as they strive to become the man that God has ordained. Give them love, strength and power. Give them a heart after God's heart. Help them to submit to living a Godly life for the sole purpose and plan of God. May God get all the glory out of their lives. In Jesus name we pray. Amen.

Key Scripture: Therefore, my beloved brethren, be steadfast, immovable, always abounding in the work of the Lord, forasmuch as ye know that your labor is not in vain in the Lord. 1 Corinthians 15:58

Objective: After reading this chapter, you should be able to identify the top issues impacting men and issues that disproportionally affect men. Understand the role of men in the church, what is true masculinity, what does the bible say about men and helpful resources.

Top Issues Impacting Men

In T.D. Jakes book entitled "He-Motions," Jakes nails the issues and challenges that Christian men face today in trying to fulfill their many roles and purse their dreams. Jakes provides a vivid description of his motivation for writing the book: "I want to share what I've learned and cut through the junk imposed on men and get to the root by talking heart to heart about what it really means to be a man in an honest, soul bearing way, which also respects men and honors the women who love them." Jakes focus is primarily geared toward the male readers but also targets the female reader who desires to gain knowledge and insight about men. Jakes provides a vivid description of men struggling internally and the women in their lives having no clue as to what is going on or how men feel about things.

It is a common belief that men don't understand women and vice versa women don't particularly understand men or rather their behaviors. We must acknowledge that in order for men to move on from the past, men must first understand their past, why it happened and how it happened. We understand the daily challenges that men face in the home, at work and even in the church. We are consistently reminded of the things that men want, things that they don't want, how they feel and even their fears. After reading this book, you will be able to better interpret men silence and uncover the myths that men have created around themselves. Life can be a struggle for both men and women. However, women have a tendency to shake it off quicker, perhaps due to their emotional behavior linked with crying and screaming. To the contrary, some men have a tendency to grow bitter rather than better and hold on to past hurts. On the exterior, most men may appear to be strong and in complete control, however, many men are struggling internally with serious issues that are beyond their control.

Top Issues that Disproportionally Affect Men

1. Building fellowship; reconnecting to meaningful and supportive fellowship with each other.
2. Fatherhood Support; Father's rights, the problem of fathers being asked to "pay and stay away," Greater fairness towards men in child custody cases.
3. Mentoring; having a mentor, allowing men to contribute to each other or being a mentor. Establishing apprenticeship and mentor programs for young men.
4. Male Depression and suicide prevention; Identification and offering compassionate non-drug and complementary treatment alternatives and education. Depression and suicide affects people of all age, color, race and creed.
5. Male sexuality; issues dealing with shame around sexuality, psychological & emotional components. Dealing with sex drive vs being driven by it. Concern about the practice of routine circumcision as cruel to male children. Reproductive rights regarding men's birth control techniques or women lying that they have used birth control to have a child. Men's input on abortion.
6. Men's health issues; prostate cancer, heart attacks, mental illness, etc.
7. How to honor and respect your partner without compromising your own self values
8. Coping with anger issues.
9. The notion of buying love. Paying for companionship
10. Having a "best" male friend, a true friend that men can trust.
11. Men supporting each other in spiritual growth

12. The importance of play and creating joy in life. The ability to laugh at yourselves.
13. Resolving relationship issues
14. Domestic violence and/or physical abuse to and from others. Men are more likely to be involved in serious crimes such as murder and are more likely to be both the perpetrator and victims of violent crime, more likely to join gangs and get arrested.
15. Addictions to drugs, alcohol, sex, lying, cheating, stealing, gambling or pornography.
16. Homelessness; statistics reveal that nearly 70% of all homelessness are men.
17. Masculinity; damaging notions of men masculinity. Teaching boys to be rough, tough, lash out and to hide their emotions rather than dealing with issues face on.

Men and the Church

Have you ever wondered or asked yourself the question "Where are the men?" If you answered yes, then you're not alone. This question has often perplexed men and women all over the world. There is no easy answer to this relevant question, however, the overarching principle may be as simple as the fact that men are institutionalized, deceased, and among us simply looking for an environment that is consistent with who they are in terms of their manhood. Moreover, men often search for an outlet where they feel comfortable in their quest to become all that God has ordained them to be. As such, men are looking for relevance. Contrary to the truth, many men do not see the value in going to church because they feel that the church is not speaking their language and that the church does not address everyday issues regarding men masculinity, guilt, sexuality, healthy marriages, raising children, work and integrity.

Men are searching for answers to questions such as: What is true masculinity? How is success measured? How do I deal with feelings of guilt and shame? What is male sexuality? How do I avoid infidelity issues? What is a healthy marriage? How do I raise my children to be successful and God fearing? How can I be a man of integrity in the workplace? How can I be a great leader at home, church and in the workplace? What is my purpose in life? Studies have shown that men want to be involved in a greater cause than themselves, they want to win in every aspect of life and they want to be heroes to their children and great husbands to their wives.

While, men tend to be competitive creatures, they are also risk takers. Most importantly, they seek a sense of belonging, adventure, change, and competition. Men measure themselves by productivity and gain a portion of self-image based on what they do and how well they do it. Their desire for adventure is often expressed in the desire to be on the solution end of things. Men want to be equipped to lead and their heart's desire is to follow a strong, bold, successful, humble, courageous, and visionary leader. Men are looking for brotherhood acquaintances, someone that they can consider as a genuine friend. They are looking to laugh and have fun in order to balance their reality. They love a good laugh, a funny joke, story, movie and sports. Men are looking for healing from present and past pain. They are seeking ways to heal from addictions, sexual misuse, drugs or alcohol.

In order for men to truthfully achieve healthy relationships and become the man that God wants them to be, they must discover healthy ways to deal with these internal wounds and deep-rooted hurts. I submit to you that Jesus is the answer and seeking God first and His righteousness, all these things will be added unto you. Matthew 6:33.

What does the Bible say about Characteristics of a Godly Man?

1. Step up and lead by example. Be a man of action and reject passivity.
    a. Be strong and let us show ourselves courageous for the sake of our people and for the cities of our God; and may the LORD do what is good in His sight. 2 Samuel 10:7, 12.
    b. I search for a man among them who would build up the wall and stand in the gap before Me for the land, so that I would not destroy it; but I found no one. Ezekiel 22:30

2. Speak Out against sin and unrighteousness. Be bold and courageous. Fear God, not man and speak truth in love.
    a. Better is open rebuke than love that is concealed. Faithful are the wounds of a friend, but deceitful are the kisses of an enemy. Proverbs 27:5-6
    b. Open your mouth, judge righteously, and defend the rights of the afflicted and needy. Proverbs 31:9
    c. Sanctify Christ as Lord in your heart, always being ready to make a defense to everyone who ask you to give an account for the hope that is in you, yet with gentleness and reverence. 1 Peter 3:15

3. Stand strong and don't give in, up or out when you face challenges, attacks or criticism.
    a. Now, behold, I have made you as a fortified city and as a pillar of iron and as walls of bronze against the whole land, to the kings of Judah, to its princes, to its priests and to the people of the land. They will fight against you, but they will not overcome you, for I am with you to deliver you declares the LORD. Jeramiah 1:18-19
    b. Therefore, my beloved brethren, be steadfast, immovable, always abounding in the work of the Lord, knowing that your toil is not in vain in the Lord. 1 Corinthians 15:58
    c. Be of a sober spirit, be on the alert because the devil, your adversary, lurks around like a roaring lion, seeking whom he may devour. But resist the Devil, be firm in your faith knowing that the same experiences of suffering are being accomplished by your brethren who are in the world. 1 Peter 5:8-9
4. Stay humble, resist pride. Don't think more highly of yourself than you ought.
    a. Let the righteous smite me in kindness and reprove me; it is oil upon the head; do not let my head refuse it, for still my prayer is against their wicked deeds. Psalm 141:5
    b. You younger men, likewise, be subject to your elders; and all of you, cloth yourselves with humility toward one another, for GOD oppose the proud but give Grace to the humble. Therefore, humble yourselves under the mighty hand of God, that He may exalt you in due time. Cast all of your cares upon Him, for He cares for you. 1 Peter 5: 5-7

5. Serve the King. Seek God's kingdom first, seek His glory and His righteousness. Hope in the Lord and live for a greater reward.
   a. But seek first His Kingdom and His righteousness and all these things will be added unto you. Matthew 6:33
   b. For even the Son of Man did not come to be served but to serve and to give His life a ransom for many. Mark 10:45.
   c. Serve the Lord with gladness, come before His presence with singing. Psalm 100:2

Knowledge Check

Please mark your answers to the following questions (T) true or (F) false.

1. T/F In order for men to move on from their past, they must first understand their friends, why it happened and how it happened.

2. T/F On the external, many men may appear to be strong and in control. Internally, they may be struggling with serious issues that are beyond their control

3. T/F Men want to be involved in a greater cause than themselves, they want to win in every aspect of life and they want to be heroes to their children and great husbands to their wives.

Helpful Resources

Connect with the Men's Ministry at your local Church

He-Motions: Even Strong Men Struggle
T.D. Jakes
http://www.thepottershouse3.org
Amazon.com

Chapter Eight
Love, Sex & Marriage

A Prayer for Marriage

Father God, in the name of Jesus, I come boldly before the throne of grace. I come giving You praise, glory and honor. I come lifting up marriages everywhere. I rebuke the spirit of discord, discontent and division in marriages. I pray that You will bless and anoint the marriages of men and women all over this nation. Teach them how to love, honor, respect, and cherish each other. Never let them grow so far apart that You can't bring them back together again. Allow their cup to run over with blessings and favor. Bless their home, health, marriage, children, jobs and finances. We thank You and we claim it as done, in Jesus name we pray. Amen.

Key Scripture: Nevertheless, let every one of you in particular so love his wife even as himself; and the wife see that she reverences her husband. Ephesians 5:33

Objective: After reading this chapter regarding marriage you should be able to identify seven practical keys for a successful marriage, issues that could potentially cause conflict in a marriage, 101 reasons to love your spouse, helpful resources and discover what the Bible says about marriage.

Marriage

A good wife is the most precious treasure a man can find. He should show her respect and praise her in public. Proverbs 31:10. He should love, honor, nourish, cherish and support her at all times.

Marriage is honorable before the Lord and is a commitment between a man and a woman. The two are joined together in holy matrimony whereas they are no longer two, but one. They are one in the Spirit and one in unity with God. What God has joined together, let no man put asunder. Mark 10:8-9.

In the 2nd Chapter of Genesis, the man refers to the woman as "bone of my bones and flesh of my flesh." These scriptures provide a clear guide and instructions on how a man and women should relate to each other. Hence, the husbands are to love their wives even as Christ also loved the church and gave Himself for it. Ephesians 5:21. And, likewise, wives are to submit (out of reverence for Christ) themselves unto their own husbands as unto the Lord. Ephesians 5:22.

Seven Practical Keys for a Successful Marriage

1. Love
   a. And beyond all these things put on love, which is the perfect bond of unity. Colossians 3:14
   b. So husbands ought also to love their own wives as their own bodies. He who loves his own wife loves himself; for no one ever hated his own flesh, but nourishes and cherishes it, just as Christ also does the church. Ephesians 5:28-29.
   c. Love is patient, love is kind and is not jealous; love does not brag and is not arrogant, does not behave unbecomingly; it does not seek its own, is not provoked, does not take into account a wrong suffered, does not rejoice in unrighteousness, but rejoices with the truth, bears all things, believes all things, hopes all things, endures all things. Love never fails, but if there are gifts of prophecy, they will be done away. 1 Corinthians 13:4-8.
   d. Nevertheless, let every one of you in particular so love his wife even as himself; and the wife see that she reverence her husband. Ephesians 5:33.
2. Sex
   a. Marriage is honorable in all, and the bed undefiled: but whoremongers and adulterers God will judge. Hebrews 13:4

3. Trust
    a. But you say "Why does he not?" Because the LORD was witness between you and the wife of your youth to whom you have been faithless, though she is your companion and your wife by covenant. Malachi 2:14, 15.
    b. Trust in the Lord with all of your heart and lean not unto your own understanding but in all your ways acknowledge him and he will direct your path. Proverbs 3:5.
4. Commitment
    a. Marriage by God's design is the union of one man and one woman. Genesis 2:18.
    b. For the woman which hath a husband is bound by the law to her husband as long as he liveth; but if the husband be dead, she is loosed from the law of her husband. Romans 7:2.
5. Communication
    a. Communication is the key to a successful marriage. It is a two-way channel. Husbands and wives should always keep the doors of communication open.
6. Honesty
    a. Be honest with your partner and do not deceive him or her. Refrain from dishonest behavior. Will ye steal, murder, commit adultery, swear falsely, burn incense unto Baal, and walk after other gods whom ye know not. Jeremiah 7:9.
7. Passion
    a. Be passionate toward one another. Desire excitement, joy, zeal and enthusiasm.

Issues That Could Potentially Cause Conflict in a Marriage

Social Media Addiction – Do you spend more time and attention surfing Facebook, Instagram, Twitter and your smartphone?

Avoiding Sex – Do you constantly make excuses to avoid being intimate with your spouse?

Communication – Good communication includes listening and communicating your needs, don't expect the other person to read your mind.

Your spouse is not your enemy – If you've had a stressful day at work, let your spouse know that it's been a difficult day. Avoid being critical and defensive.

Financial Planning – In a 2013 study conducted by Kansas State University regarding couples finances, it was discovered that one major contributing factor of divorce is couples arguing about money. Talk openly with your spouse about how money is spent and how much will be saved. Avoid large purchases that you do not discuss with your spouse in advance.

Avoid Extra Marital Relationships – Don't allow other relationships to take priority over your spouse. When you get married, you and your spouse becomes one. Your spouse should come first before your children, relatives and friends.

Fight Fair – The way in which you settle or resolve your differences can either solidify or tear down your relationship with your spouse. Develop respect, and trust.

Helpful Guide

- Don't always try to be right; instead try to resolve the problem
- Consider your partner's point of view; keep an open mind
- Solve one problem at a time
- Don't bring up past issues
- Avoid personal attacks and criticism
- Don't use guilt, threats and emotional blackmail
- Don't avoid each other after an argument or disagreement
- Apologize and make up
- Don't forget the little things
- Write love notes or send a text message
- Demonstrate acts of kindness
- Don't forget to say I Love You
- Provide reassurance and affirmations
- Get intimate, close and offer loving gestures
- Assist with completing a task that your spouse hates

Why Do I Love You? Let Me Count the Ways

1. I love the way we finish each other's sentences.

2. I love the way I know you'll never give up on me.

3. I love the fact that I wouldn't ever give up on you.

4. I love the way you look at me.

5. I love how beautiful your eyes are.

6. I love the way that I can't imagine a day without you in my life.

7. I love the way that if we were ever separated I wouldn't know how to go on.

8. I love the way we cuddle and watch sunsets together.

9. I love the way we sometimes stay up all night and just talk, then watch the sunrise together.

10. I love how I know you'll always be there when I need you to be.

11. I love the fact that I will always be there for you, too.

12. I love how when I dream of my life partner, the only person that I can see is you.

13. I love how complete I feel when I am with you.

14. I love how our bodies just fit together.

15. I love the way you make me laugh.

16. I love the way you laugh.

17. I love the way you won't compromise yourself when we are together.

18. I love the way you won't let me compromise myself.

19. I love your thoughtfulness.

20. I love your tenderness.

21. I love your ability to speak without saying a single word.

22. I love the way we glance at each other across the room and know what each other is thinking.

23. I love the way, how even though we may be miles apart I still feel like you're right here with me.

24. I love the way you surprise me with the perfect gifts that show you pay attention to me.

25. I love the way you'll watch a sporting game with me even though you may not be interested in it.

26. I love the way you treat my friends.

27. I love your love for the things that interest me.

28. I love the way you let me live my life freely without jealousy.

29. I love how you demand respect, but are not controlling.

30. I love how I would do anything in this world to make you happy.

31. I love how you would do anything in this world to make me happy.

32. I love the way your voice sounds over the phone.

33. I love the way your voice sounds when you whisper sweet nothings in my ear.

34. I love the completeness and oneness I feel when we make love.

35. I love your sensuality.

36. I love how our romance feels like the perfect romance movie.

37. I love how you are my soul mate.

38. I love the way you handle troubled times.

39. I love the way you respect me.

40. I love the way you protect and defend me.

41. I love how you feel when we cuddle.

42. I love the softness of your lips against mine.

43. I love the softness of your lips against my body.

44. I love the feeling of your hair brushing against me when we make love.
45. I love lying in bed at night talking about nothing.

46. I love waking up to find we've been cuddling together all night.

47. I love the surprises you leave for me.

48. I love your intelligence.

49. I love your ingenuity.

50. I love your ability to make friends where ever we go.

51. I love your love for life.

52. I love your passion for your hobbies and interests.

53. I love how every time I look at you, you take my breath away.

54. I love how I thank God every day for bringing someone as wonderful as you into my life.

55. I love the fact you gave me the gift of our children.

56. I love the special moments that we shared that will remain my fondest memories of you and I.

57. I love spending the holidays with the one person I love the most.

58. I love how my heart skips a beat whenever you walk into the room.

59. I love how you love me.

60. I love how I love you.

61. I love the ways you choose to show your affection for me.

62. I love the way you inspire me to be more than I am.

63. I love the way you spark my creativity and imagination.

64. I love the way you make me feel like anything is possible as long as I'm with you.

65. I love your sense of humor.

66. I love the way you make me feel like royalty.

67. I love the way you dress.

68. I love your understated elegance.

69. I love you just the way you are.

70. I love your spontaneity.

71. I love our life together.

72. I love how if I died right now, I would be the happiest person alive knowing I found my one true love.

73. I love the fact that we will grow old together.

74. I love your way with words.

75. I love the way you look when you're sleeping.

76. I love the way you think you look awful when you first wake up when it is actually then I find you the most beautiful.

77. I love your willingness to share everything and most especially your heart with me.

78. I love your strength of character.

79. I love taking showers together.

80. I love the way you leave me love notes to find whenever you're gone.

81. I love the way you treat me.

82. I love the way you take care of us.

83. I love your cooking.

84. I love the way you take the time to thank me for doing everyday things.

85. I love the way you show your affection when we are around friends and/or family.

86. I love the way you are not scared to show your affection when we are in public.

87. I love your confidence.

88. I love your ability to make me feel better when times are tough.

89. I love the way we make up after a fight.

90. I love how you treat our children.

91. I love the way you support me when I'm off track.

92. I love the way you take the time to show me how much you love me.

93. I love your beautiful hair.

94. I love your body.

95. I love your openness to try new things.

96. I love your ability to talk things through.

97. I love your courage to be you.

98. I love your greatness.

99. I love the fact that you want to be with me and only me.

100 I love the way you make me feel when I am with you.

101 I love you just for being you.

What does the Bible say about Marriage?

Because of the temptation to sexual immorality, each man should have his own wife and each woman her own husband. 1 Corinthians 7:2
Now concerning sin, flee adultery, uncleanness, lasciviousness. Live soberly by "denying ungodliness and worldly lusts, we should live soberly, righteously and godly in the present age, looking for the blessed hope and glorious appearing of our great God and Savior Jesus Christ." Titus 2:12-13
A lustful look at a woman is sinful "whosoever looketh on a woman to lust after her hath committed adultery with her already in his heart." Matthew 5:28
Two are better than one because they have a good return for their labor. For if either of them falls, the one will lift up the companion. But woe to the one who falls when there is not another to lift him up. Furthermore, if two lie down together they keep warm, but how can one be warm alone? And if one can overpower him who is alone, two can resist him. A cord of three stands is not quickly torn apart. Ecclesiastes 4:9-12
Love is patient, love is kind, and is not jealous; love does not brag and is not arrogant, does not act unbecomingly; it does not seek its own, is not easily provoked, does not take into account a wrong suffered, does not rejoice in unrighteousness, but rejoices in the truth; bears all things, believes all things, hopes all things, endures all things. Love never fails; but if there are gifts of prophecy, they will be done away; if there are tongues, they will cease; if there is knowledge, it will be done away. 1 Corinthians 13:4-8

A Bishop then must be blameless, the husband of one wife, vigilant, sober, of good behavior, given to hospitality, apt to teach. 1 Timothy 3:2

Husbands love your wives just as Christ also loved the church and gave Himself up for her; that He might sanctify her, having cleansed her by the washing of water with the word, that He might present to Himself the church in all her glory, having no spot or wrinkle or any such thing; but that she should be holy and blameless. So husbands aught also to love their own wives as their own bodies. He who loves his own wife loves himself; for no one ever hated his own flesh, but nourishes and cherishes it, just as Christ also does the church. Ephesians 5:25-29

In the same way, you wives, be submissive to your own husbands so that even if any of them are disobedient to the word, they may be won without a word by the behavior of their wives, as they observe your chaste and respectful behavior. And let not your adornment be merely external, braiding the hair and wearing gold jewelry or putting on dresses; but let it be the hidden person of the heart, with the imperishable quality of a gentle and quiet spirit, which is precious in the sight of God. For in this way in former times the holy women also, who hoped in God, used to adorn themselves, being submissive to their own husbands. Thus Sarah obeyed Abraham, calling him Lord and you have become her children if you do what is right without being frightened by any fear.
1 Peter 3:1-6

Marriage by God's design is the union of one man and one woman.
Genesis 2:18

So the LORD God caused a deep sleep to fall upon the man and while he slept took one of his ribs and closed up its place with flesh. And the rib that the LORD God had taken from the man he made into a woman and brought her to the man. Then the man said, "This at last is bone of my bone and flesh of my flesh; she shall be called Woman, because she was taken out of Man." Therefore, a man shall leave his father and his mother and hold fast to his wife and they shall become one flesh. And the man and his wife were both naked and were not ashamed. Genesis 2:21-25

But you say, "Why does he not?" Because the LORD was witness between you and the wife of your youth, to whom you have been faithless, though she is your companion and your wife by covenant. Malachi 2:14-15

Let marriage be held in honor among all, and let the marriage bed be undefiled, for God will judge the sexually immoral and adulterous. Hebrew 13:4

But whoso committeth adultery with a woman lacketh understanding: he that doeth it destroyeth his own soul. Proverbs 6:32

But I say unto you, that whosoever looketh on a woman to lust after her hath committed adultery with her already in his heart. Matthew 5:28

Marriage is honorable in all and the bed undefiled: but whoremongers and adulterers God will judge. Hebrews 13:4

And I say unto you, whosoever shall put away his wife, except it be for fornication, and shall marry another, committeth adultery: and whoso marrieth her which is put away doth commit adultery. Matthew 19:9

To keep thee from the evil woman, from the flattery of the tongue of a strange woman. Proverbs 6:24

Thou salt not commit adultery. Exodus 20:14

For this ye know that no whoremonger, nor unclean person, nor covetous man who is an idolater hath any inheritance in the kingdom of Heaven. Ephesians 5:5

There hath no temptation taken you but such as is common to man: but God is faithful, who will not suffer you to be tempted above that ye are able; but will with the temptation also make a way to escape, that ye may be able to bear it. 1 Corinthians 10:13

They say unto Him, Master, this woman was taken in adultery, in the very act. John 8:4

Now the works of the flesh are manifest, which are these: Adultery, fornication, uncleanness, lasciviousness. Galatians 5:19

And if a woman shall put away her husband and be married to another, she committeth adultery. Mark 10:12

For the lips of a strange woman drop as a honeycomb and her mouth is smoother than oil. Proverbs 5:3

And if a man entice a maid that is not betrothed and lie with her, he shall surely endow her to be his wife. Exodus 22:16
Will ye steal, murder, commit adultery, swear falsely, burn incense unto Baal and walk after other gods whom ye know not? Jeremiah 7:9
For the woman which hath a husband is bound by the law to her husband so long as he liveth; but if the husband be dead, she is loosed from the law of her husband. Romans 7:2
Let the husband render unto his wife due benevolence; and likewise also the wife unto the husband. 1 Corinthians 7:3-5

Helpful Resources

American Association for Marriage & Family Therapy   703-838-9808
www.aamft.org

Enrichment Journal   417-862-2781 ext. 4095 or 1-800-641-4310
www.enrichmentjournal.ag.org

Marriage Fitness with Mort Fertel   410-764-1552
www.marriagemax.com

Knowledge Check

Please mark your answers to the following questions (T) true or (F) false.

1. T/F   Marriage is honorable before the Lord and is a commitment between a man and a woman

2. T/F   Based on scripture, husbands are to love their wives as Christ also loved the church and gave himself for it and wives are to submit themselves unto their own husbands as unto the Lord.

3. T/F   Good communication includes listening and communicating your needs to your partner rather than expecting the other person to read your mind.

Chapter Nine
Singles

A Prayer for Singles

Father God, in the name of Jesus, I come before You today lifting up single men and women. I pray that You will give them a sense of security and peace in who they are in You. Help them to discover their true purpose in life. Help them to understand that they do not need someone else to make them whole or complete and that they are complete in You alone. May they embrace and accept the truth that they were created to praise and worship You as You continue to bless them until You send their special sole mate. We thank You and we praise You, in Jesus name we pray. Amen.

Key Scripture: Now to the unmarried and the widows I say: it is good for them to stay unmarried, as I do. But if they cannot control themselves, they should marry, for it is better to marry than to burn with passion. 1 Corinthians 8-9 (NIV)

Objective: After reading this chapter on singles, you should be able to identify what it means to be single, understand the dating process and marriage, identify the top five characteristics of a potential partner, and identify what the Bible says about being single and helpful resources.

Who is considered a single person?

A single person is defined as someone who is not in a relationship or one who is unmarried. The term single refers to only one, solitary, sole or alone. 63% of our population are single. One out of every three are Christians. Being in a society where the joy of premarital sex is often emphasized, many single Christians struggle with issues ranging from loneliness and unfulfilled desires to self-control and self-worth.

The Bible explains that single women should be concerned about the things of the Lord. Do not allow yourself to become so pre-occupied with getting married that you miss your purpose in life. ***God wants to be number one in your life! God wants an intimate relationship with you!*** God wants you to be pure and to wait on the Him. Be aware that temptation will come, but God will not allow you to be tempted above which you are able to escape. Remember that God is a jealous God and He does not want to share you with anyone else. God wants to use you in your singleness and while some people choose to remain single for an extended period of time, many singles are actively engaged in seeking meaningful relationships via social media outlets such as Facebook, Instagram, Match.com, and Christiansmingles.com to name a few. While these social media outlets can be successful for some individuals, many may be extremely high risk and unsafe.

Amazingly, some singles even struggle with feelings of "incompleteness." **You are complete in Christ!** *Know who you are in Christ and that you do not need someone else to complete you.* Many singles may feel that their life has no meaning or value and that God cannot use them. These emotional highs and lows are lies from the enemy and often lead to premature connections resulting in unequally yoked partners. *The Bible tells us to seek the Kingdom of God and His righteousness first then all other things will be added unto us, that includes our soul mate.*

Top Five Characteristics of a Potential Partner:

1. Love God
2. Honor and Respect
3. Financially Stability
4. Self Confidence
5. Good Communicator

When considering a lifetime partner, you should be aware that excessive arguing and/or abusive behavior early on in a relationship are red flags. Hence, you should terminate the relationship immediate before it's too late. *Above all; guard your heart for it is the wellspring of life. Proverbs 4:23.*

In terms of marriage and long term commitment, remember that marriage is honorable before God. So, wait on the Lord. Do not rush or feel pressured into getting married because of social norms. There are no specific age or timeline requirements for marriage. You are not desperate nor in despair.

In terms of motherhood and having children, that, too, can be delayed as an increasing number of women are choosing to get pregnant and have babies beyond the age of 40. Don't rush parenthood, instead plan in advance and wait on the Lord and He will give you the desires of your heart.

God knows what is best for you. Allow His will for your life to be done. Trust in the Lord, seek His face and accept His perfect will for your life!

What does the Bible say about Singleness?

Now to the unmarried and the widows I say: It is good for them to stay unmarried, as I do, but if they cannot control themselves, they should marry, for it is better to marry than to burn with passion. I Corinthians 7:8-9
I have loved you with an everlasting love, therefore I have continued by faithfulness to you. Jeremiah 3:13
I will make you like my signet ring, for I have chosen you. Haggai 2:23
You will be called Sought After. Isaiah 62:12
You are precious and honored in my sight. Isaiah 43:4
I have engraved you on the palms of my hands. Isaiah 49:16
And lest, when I come again, my God will humble me among you and that I shall bewail many which have sinned already, and have not repented of the uncleanness and fornication and lasciviousness which they have committed. 2 Corinthians 12:21
For God hath not called us unto uncleanness, but unto holiness. 1 Thessalonians 4:7
For this is the will of God, even your sanctification, that ye should abstain from fornication. 1 Thessalonians 4:3-5

Know ye not that your bodies are the members of Christ? Shall I then take the members of Christ and make them the members of an harlot? God forbid. 1 Corinthians 6:15-18
Meats for the belly and the belly for meats: but God shall destroy both it and them. Now the body is not for fornication but for the Lord; and the Lord for the body. 1 Corinthians 6:13
For a whore is a deep ditch; and a strange woman is a narrow pit. Proverbs 23
Even as Sodom and Gomorrah and the cities about them in like manner, giving themselves over to fornication and going after strange flesh are set forth for an example, suffering the vengeance of eternal fire. Jude 1:7
Mortify therefore your members which are upon the earth; fornication, uncleanness, evil, covetousness and idolatry Colossians 3:5
Flee fornication. Every sin that a man doeth is without the body; but he that committeth fornication sinneth against his own body. 1 Corinthians 6:18

Helpful Resource:

Connect with your Christian Single's Ministry at your local Church.

Some singles have connected to Christianmingles.com for on line dating.

When we're alone with God, there are no more distractions to the development of Intimacy, it is just us and Him, The rest of the world must wait.
Wellington Boone

Knowledge Check

Please mark your answers to the following questions (T) true or (F) false.

1. T/F A single person is defined as someone who is in a relationship with another person.

2. T/F Many single Christians struggle with issues ranging from loneliness and unfulfilled desires to self-control and self-worth

3. T/F Excessive arguing and/or abusive behavior in a relationship are red flags. You should terminate the relationship immediate.

Chapter Ten
Bullying

A Prayer for Bullying

Father God, in the precious name of Jesus, I pray for all the boys and girls and even men and women that may be experiencing bullying (to include cyber bullying). Bullying of any sort is an ungodly act and does not align with the Word and the will of God. For God is love. Therefore, I come against and denounce tormenting spirits and any spirit that is not of God. Today, I release into the atmosphere God's love, peace, and protection over the victims of bullying. I declare and decree that the atmosphere is free of bullying. Most importantly, I denounce bullying in our schools, and the workplace. I declare today that the people of God has been set free from the strongholds of bullying, persecution, and harassment. Spirit of darkness cease and flee from God's people. Devil, I serve notice on you today that you are defeated in the name of Jesus. I give God all the praise, glory and honor, in Jesus name I pray. Amen.

Key Scripture: Be strong and of a good courage, fear not, nor be afraid of them: for the LORD thy God, he it is that doth go with thee; he will not fail thee, nor forsake thee. Deuteronomy 31:6

Objective: After reading this chapter you should be able to identify the true meaning of bullying, why do people bully others, what to do if you are or you know someone that is being bullied, helpful resources, what does the Bible say about bullying.

Stop Bullying

What is bullying?
Bullying is the use of superior strength or influence to intimidate someone, typically to force him or her to do what one wants. ***Bullying is unwanted aggressive behavior that involves a perceived power imbalance.*** Bullying is hurtful physically, mentally, and emotionally. *Bullying comes in the form of physical, verbal, and cyber bullying.*

One of the main reasons people bully others is to gain control. Hence, they are unhappy, insecure and suffer from low self- esteem. It is noteworthy to mention that the perpetrator may be or have been in the past a victim of bully. People that bully others often feel worthless and devalued. Their ultimate goal is to cause you feel as worthless and miserable as they are feeling. Of course, you are familiar with the saying "misery loves company". Yes, misery does love company and in this particular case you just happen to be that "company". Perhaps, now you are asking yourself "why me?" That's a good question. However, research has proven that perpetrators strategically choose their victims and prey on their emotions and vulnerability. Bullying is about a power imbalance and control. The perpetrator lacks control in some area (s) of their life and they seek to regain that control. The perpetrator will persistently bully their victim by inflicting pain as a public display of cruelty. The Bible teaches us in Deuteronomy 31:6 to *"Be Strong."* It's not easy to be strong, but you don't have to go through it alone. *Remember, **your strength comes from the LORD**!* When you are weak, God's strength is manifested. Consider the story of how David defeated Goliath with a sling shot, a rock and help from the Lord! ***You, too, can defeat your giant (bullying) with help from the Lord!***

Bullying – A Sign of Power Imbalance

Power imbalance comes from three sources:

- ✓ *Popularity*
- ✓ *Strength*
- ✓ *Cognitive ability*

Most kids do not tell adults or others about the bullying due to fear of being teased by peers, perceived as weak or a tattletale, embarrassed, backlash, humiliation, social isolation, rejection, loss of friends, and wanting to be able to control the situation. You must *tell and report*.

Three types of Bullying

1. ***Verbal bullying*-** Teasing, name calling, inappropriate sexual comments, taunting, threatening to cause harm.

2. ***Social bullying*-** Hurting someone's repetition, excluding someone on purpose, telling others not to be friends, spreading rumors, embarrassing in public.

3. ***Physical bullying*-** Hitting/kicking/pinching, spitting, tripping/pushing, stealing or destroying someone else's possessions, rude or mean gestures.

Warning Signs
Unexplainable injuries
Lost items (books, clothes)
Frequent headaches and stomach aches
Change in eating habits
Difficulty sleeping
Nightmares
Declining grades
Refusal to attend school
Loss of friends and inability to make new friends
Lack of interest in social events
Decrease in self-esteem
Feelings of helplessness
Self-destructive behavior
Running away from home
Talking about suicide
Fighting

High Risk Factors

Perceived as different from the norm, weight, dress, perceived as weak, depressed, anxious, low self-esteem, few friends, difficulties in getting alone with others.

Ending Results if not resolved

The victim may experience excessive weight loss or gain, low self-esteem, difficulties sleeping, increased isolation, rejection, exclusion, despair, anxiety, distrust of others, loneliness, depression, substance abuse, and even suicide.

Bullying Statistics

In 2014-2015, The National Center for Education Statistics and Bureau of Justices Statistics reported that 21% of children ages 12-18 experienced bullying in school and 20% of children in grades 9-12 experienced bullying in school. 30% of children admit they have bullied others, 70.6% admit to witnessing bullying and 70.4% of school staff have admitted to witnessing bullying in school. Middle school students are among the highest group of children experiencing verbal and social bullying. Bullying usually stops within 10 seconds 57% of the time when bystanders intervene. It has been reported that a zero tolerance and expulsion from school are not effective approaches.

Anti-Bullying Facts

While there are currently no Federal anti-bullying laws, 49 States have adopted anti-bullying legislation. Some States have adopted both laws and policies while others have adopted only policies. Bullying is not a Federal crime, however, when bullying turns into harassment, it becomes illegal and breaks Federal Law. Contrary to popular belief, bullying among college students and adults are not referred to as "bullying" but rather as hazing, stalking, and harassment.

Helpful Tips

If you or someone that you know are experiencing bullying:

1. Don't respond to the cyber bullying
2. Tell someone. If you are a child, communicate with a parent
3. Report the incident(s) to school officials and your local police authority
4. Don't be embarrassed or ashamed to tell someone. After all, you have not done anything wrong to cause the behavior.
5. When reported, the offender will likely stop the bullying and could be persecuted in a court of law.

If a child is being bullied in school, you should contact the following:

1. Teacher
2. School Counselor
3. School Principal
4. School Superintendent
5. State Department of Education
6. U.S. Department of Education- Civil Rights Div.
7. U.S. Department of Justice- Civil Rights Div.

What does the Bible say about Bullying?

Whosoever hateth his brother is a murderer: and ye know that no murderer hath eternal life abiding in him. 1 John 3:15
Blessed are ye, when men shall revile you and persecute you and shall say all manners of evil against you falsely for my sake. Matthew 5:11
I will call upon the LORD, who is worthy to be praised: so shall I be saved from mine enemies. Psalms 18:3
Behold, all they that were incensed against thee shall be ashamed and confounded: they shall be as nothing: and they that strive with thee shall perish. Isaiah 41:11-13.
Behold, they shall surely gather together, but not by me: whosoever shall gather together against thee shall fall for thy sake. Isaiah 54:15-17.
Be strong and of a good courage, fear not, nor be afraid of them: for the LORD thy God, he it is that doth go with thee; he will not fail thee, nor forsake thee. Deuteronomy 31:6
For I know the thoughts that I think toward you, saith the LORD, thoughts of peace, and not of evil, to give you an expected end. Jeremiah 29:11
My help cometh from the LORD, which made heaven and earth. Psalms 121:2.
For God hath not given us the spirit of fear; but of power, and of love, and of a sound mind. 2 Timothy 1:7

Helpful Resources for Bullying

Bullying Prevention Hotline   205-329-5154
www.bullyinghotline.org

Bullying Hotline   1-800-784-2433
www.stopbullying.gov

National Center for Victims of Crime 202-467-8700
www.victimsofcrime.org

24hr Bullying hotline   1-800-273-TALK

Trevor Lifeline (LGBTQ)   1-866-4-U-Trevor

Stop Bullying.gov   911
www.stopbullying.gov

National Suicide Prevention   1-800-273-8255

Knowledge Check

Please mark your answers to the following questions (T) true or (F) false.

1. T/F Bullying comes in the form of physical, verbal and cyber bullying

2. T/F One of the main reasons people bully others is to gain control and a power imbalance

3. T/F Research has shown that perpetrators strategically choose their victims and prey on their emotions and vulnerability

Chapter Eleven
Peer Pressure

A Prayer for those Experiencing Peer Pressure
Father God, in the name of Jesus, I come before Your presence today lifting up boys and girls all over the world that may be experiencing negative influences and peer pressure. Father, I pray that You will help them to make the right decisions in life. Help them to understand that they are leaders and not followers. Allow them to embrace their own uniqueness, talents, abilities and self-identify. Help them to make wise decisions as it relates to drugs, alcohol, crime, sex and bullying. Thank You for blessing our children and for equipping them with the mindset to resist negative behavior and temptations. We give You all the praise, glory and honor, in Jesus name we pray. Amen.

Key Scripture: And be not conformed to this world; but be ye transformed by the renewing of your mind, that ye may prove what is that good, and acceptable and perfect will of God. Romans 12:2

Objective: After reading this chapter you should be able to identify the signs of negative verses positive peer pressure, strategies to assist youth in dealing with peer pressure, what the Bible says about peer pressure, and helpful resources.

What is Peer Pressure?

Most of our children will experience peer pressure at some point in their lives. Consequently, peer pressure can come in the form of convincing someone to conform to or to do the "cool" thing that goes against family values and morals. *While peer pressure can be either negative or positive, it is important to mention that negative peer pressure can often lead to high risk, unhealthy and unsafe behaviors.* Some of the more recognizable signs of negative peer pressure include but are not limited to: low self-esteem, a desire to want to be someone else, a decrease in self-control, substance abuse and/or misconduct, and depression.

To the contrary, positive peer pressure can be beneficial to a child in terms of developing increased self-esteem, working harder in school and rejecting drugs, sex and alcohol abuse. In addition, positive peer pressure allows youth to feel more accepted and develop a sense of belonging. Parents who include youth and adolescents in the decision making process have discovered that they have developed a closer relationship and a more significant influence on their child's life. Moreover, they may observe that their child is developing greater leadership abilities to include thinking more independently and embracing their own ideas.

Strategies to help your teen resist negative peer pressure

- ✓ Encourage positive peer relationships
- ✓ Nurture teen's abilities and self-esteem to equip them to foster positive relationships and deflect negative peer pressure.
- ✓ Encourage diverse relationships
- ✓ Take a stand against bullying
- ✓ Equip youth, teens and adolescence with the tools necessary to resist negative behaviors
- ✓ Encourage good decisions
- ✓ Teach exit strategies
- ✓ Encourage them to just say "No"
- ✓ Own your identity

Knowledge Check

Please mark your answers to the following questions (T) true or (F) false.

1. T/F   Peer pressure can come in the form of convincing someone to conform to or to do the "cool" thing that goes against family values and morals

2. T/F   Negative peer pressure can often lead to high risk, unhealthy and unsafe behaviors

3. T/F Positive peer pressure can help a child in developing increased self-esteem to include working harder in school and rejecting drugs, sex and alcohol abuse

What Does the Bible Say about Peer Pressure?

There hath no temptation taken you but such as is common to man; but God is faithful, who will not suffer you to be tempted above that ye are able; but will with the temptation also make a way to escape that ye may be able to bear it. 1 Corinthians 10:13
And be not conformed to this world; but be ye transformed by the renewing of your mind, that ye may prove what is that good, and acceptable and perfect will of God. Romans 12:2
Be not deceived; evil communications corrupt good manners. 1 Corinthians 12:33
My son, if sinners entice thee, consent thou not. Proverbs 1:10
For do I now persuade men, or God? Or do I seek to please men? For if I yet pleased men, I should not be the servant of Christ. Galatians 1:10
Then Peter and the other apostles answered and said, we ought to obey God rather than men. Acts 5:29

Blessed is the man that endured temptation: for when he is tried, he shall receive the crown of life, which the Lord hath promised to them that love him. James 1:12-15
Therefore, brethren, stand fast, and hold the traditions which ye have been taught, whether by word or our epistle. 2 Thessalonians 2:15
The fear of man bringeth a snare: but whoso putteth his trust in the LORD shall be safe. Provers 29:25.
Be ye followers of me, even as I also am of Christ. 1 Corinthians 11:1
The Lord knoweth how to deliver the godly out of temptations, and to reserve the unjust unto the Day of Judgment to be punished. 2 Peter 2:9

Helpful Resources for Peer Pressure

Adolescents' relationships with peers. In R. M. Lerner & L. Steinberg (Eds.), Handbook of Adolescent Psychology, 2nd edition (pp. 363-394) New York; Wiley. Brown, B.B. (2004).

Peer groups and peer cultures. In S. S. Feldman & G. R. Elliott (Eds.) At the threshold: The developing adolescent (pp. 171-198). Cambridge, MA: Harvard University Press. Brown, B.B. (1990)

Friendships, cliques, and crowds. In G. R. Adams & M.D. Berzonsky (Eds.) Blackwell Handbook of Adolescence (pp. 330-348) Malden, MA: Blackwell Publishing. Steinberg, L. (2005) Adolescence. New York, NY: McGraw-Hill.

Chapter Twelve
Salvation and the Church

A Prayer for Salvation

Father God, in the name of Jesus I come before Your presence today lifting up those that are lost and need a Savior. I pray that every man, woman, boy, and girl all over this world will accept You as their personal Lord and Savior. I pray that the lost will be found and that the blind will see. I pray that Your Holy Spirit will rest, rule and abide in their lives forever. Help them to look to You, to seek You, to call upon Your name and to hunger and thirst after Your righteousness. Bless every Pastor, Minister and Leader as they feed Your sheep and boldly proclaim the Word of God. Build them up where they are torn down; strengthen them where they are weak. We thank You and we give You all the Praise, Glory and Honor, in Jesus name we pray. Amen.

Key Scripture: If thou shalt confess with thy mouth the Lord Jesus, and shalt believe in thine heart that God hath raised him from the dead, thou shalt be saved. Romans 10:9

Objective: After reading this chapter on Salvation you should be able to identify the meaning of salvation, truths and myths regarding salvation, the ABCs of salvation, and scriptures relating to salvation.

For God sent not his Son into the world to condemn the world; but that the world through him might be saved. John 3:17

Salvation

What does it mean to be saved?

Being saved mean that you are delivered from the practice, penalty and power of sin. You are saved by accepting Jesus as your Lord and Savior. You are saved by the Grace of God, not by works but, rather, your faith in God. You are saved by the blood of the Jesus. Jesus paid the ultimate penalty on the Cross of Calvary over 2000 years ago. Jesus hung, bleed, and died for my sins and for your sins and for the sins of the world. John 3:16 tells us that God so loved the world that He gave His only begotten Son, that whosoever believeth in Him should not perish, but have everlasting life.

The ABC's of Salvation

A= Admit that you are a sinner
B= Believe in Christ as your Lord and Savior
C= Confess Jesus as your Lord and Savior
D= Do the things that God has commanded

<u>Repeat this Prayer of Salvation</u>: Lord God, I confess that I am a sinner. I believe that Jesus died on the Cross for my sins. I ask You Lord to forgive me of all my sins and I invite You to come into my life and save me. I accept Jesus as my Lord and Savior. In Jesus name I pray. Amen.

Congratulations! You are saved!

Let's examine some common myths surrounding salvation. Myth #1 - Many people get saved, join the church, and attend regular Sunday morning worship services and think that they will never have problems in life again. Unfortunately, that's simply not true. The truth of the matter is that you will continue to have problems, trials, and tribulations in life. You are not exempt! In fact, it's just the opposite. You are now a major target for the enemy. You are a threat to the kingdom of darkness. Satan wants you back because he knows that you have discovered the truth about God's love and the lies of the enemy. You now know that you do not have to face difficulties and challenges alone because *God is always with you and He has promised to never leave nor forsake you. In the scriptures Luke 10:19 reminds us that God has given us the power to tread over serpents and scorpions and most of all power over the enemy and nothing shall by any means hurt us.* What that means is that we can defeat our enemies and **conquer with Christ as we overcome our adversities through the Word of God!** Moreover, the Bible teaches us that there are consequences for worldly living in contrast to Godly living. *John 16:33 says "These things I have spoken unto you, that in Me ye might have peace. In the world ye shall have tribulations but be of good cheer; I have overcome the world."* Hence, submitting your life to Christ brings about peace.

As we take a look at Myth #2 - We discover that many people believe that being saved means that they will never sin again. As profound as that may sound, that's simply not true either. The truth is that we will sin again, primarily due to our sinful nature, however, we can ask God for forgiveness. We have an advocate, Jesus Christ, who will go before the Father on our behalf and plead our case. Jesus reconciles us unto the Father, therefore, we do not have to yield unto temptation or sin. Instead, when we sin, we need to repent of our sins and ask God to forgive us and to wash us so that we may be cleanse from all unrighteousness.

What does the Bible say about Salvation?

For God so loved the world, that he gave his only begotten Son, that whosoever believeth in him should not perish, but have everlasting life. John 3:16
For by grace are ye saved through faith; and that not of yourselves; it is the gift of God. Ephesians 2:8
Jesus saith unto him, I am the way, the truth, and the life: no man cometh unto the Father, but by me. John 14:6
Neither is there salvation in any other: for there is none other name under heaven given among men, whereby we must be saved. Acts 4:12
No man can come to me, except the Father which hath sent me draw him; and I will raise him up at the last day. John 6:44
I am the true vine, and my Father is the husbandman. John 15:1
I am the vine, ye are the branches: He that abideth in me and I in him, the same bringeth forth much fruit: for without me ye can do nothing. John 15:5
But the salvation of the righteous is of the LORD: he is their strength in the time of trouble. Psalms 37:39
For sin shall not have dominion over you; for ye are not under the law, but under grace. Romans 6:14

Scriptures to read during times of Despair

Anger	Proverbs 16:32
Depression	Psalms 40:1-3
Discouraged	Isaiah 40:31
Faith	Hebrews 11
Fear	Isaiah 41:10
Grief	Isaiah 61:3
Heartbroken	Psalms 147:3
Help	Psalm 121
Loneliness	Deuteronomy 31:8
Patience	Galatians 6
Sadness	Psalms 34:17-18
Sorrow	John 14
Suicide	Psalms 138:7
Temptation	1 Corinthians 10:13
Worry	1 Peter 5:7

Knowledge Check

Please mark your answers to the following questions (T) true or (F) false.

1. T/F   Being saved means that you are delivered from the practice, penalty and power of sin.

2. T/F   You are saved by your good works toward others and the Grace of God.

3. T/F   Being saved means that you will never sin again and you will no longer experience difficulties and challenges in life.

Salvation and the Church

A Prayer for the Church

Father God, in the name of Jesus, I pray that You will bless our church and every church in this Nation. Bless our Pastors, Deacons, Elders and Leaders as they boldly proclaim the Gospel of Jesus Christ to a lost world. Send an overflow of Your divine grace, power, wisdom and anointing. I pray that the anointing will break every yoke and destroy every strong hold of the enemy. Give them peace, patience, love and compassion as they effectively minister the Good News of the Gospel to the world. Keep them safe from the enemy and the powers of darkness. Let no hurt, harm or danger come near them. May they walk upright in Your sight and in the sight of men. We give You all the Praise, Glory and Honor in Jesus name we pray. Amen.

Key Scripture: Simon Peter replied, "You are the Christ, the Son of the living God." And Jesus answered him, "Blessed are you, Simon Bar-Jonah! For Flesh and blood has not revealed this to you, but my Father who is in heaven. And I tell you, you are Peter, and on this rock I will build my church, and the gates of hell shall not prevail against it. Matthew 16:16-18

Objective: After reading this chapter on The Local Church you should be able to identify the true meaning of a church and a church building, the purpose of the church, reasons why people do and do not go to church.

The Local Church

What is a Church?

We, the body of born again believers in Christ, are the church. We have been called from darkness into light.

What is not a Church?

- A Church is not a place
- A Church is not a building
- A Church is not a location
- A Church is not a denomination.

A Church building is a place used for religious activities and worship services. There are more than 37 million churches in the world and approximately 34 thousand Christian denominations. While there are several types of denominations that exist worldwide to include, but not limited to, Baptist, Catholic, Protestant, Eastern Orthodox, Lutheran, Methodist, Presbyterianism, Pentecostal, Nondenominational, Church of God in Christ (COGIC), African Initiated Protestant, Seventh Day Adventist, the Mormon, and Jehovah's Witness, we are all one in the Spirit of God and one in the Spirit of love. They will know that we are Christians by our love.

God is not concerned about our denomination, however, He is concerned about our salvation!

The Purpose of the Church

What is the true purpose of the church? The purpose of the church is two-fold:

1. *The church assembles together to worship, inspire, encourage, motivate, uplift and edify one another Ephesians 4:14*

2. *The church is called to go into the world to reach unbelievers and share the gospel of the good news of Jesus Christ Matthew 28:18-20*

Why should I attend church?

We all know that attending Church is a personal decision. Yet, it is one of the most important decisions that you will ever make in your life. Attending church is not only beneficial to your spiritual growth and development, but it is also detrimental to your overall health and wellness. For these reasons, attending church is ultimately a wise decision and it allows you the opportunity to meet, and fellowship with new people.

Moreover, we are commanded by God to assemble with believers coupled with paying a ten percent of our tithes for the advancement of the church. Malachi 3:10. In addition, we are commanded to participate in the Holy Sacraments, including Baptism and Communion according to Luke 22:14-20, Matthew 28:19-20, and John 6:48-51.

101 Reasons why People do not go to Church

1. The Church is just a building so why should I go
2. The people are not sincere, they're too fake and phony
3. The people there act too sophisticated
4. Church people think that they are better than others
5. I don't need to go to church because I am a good person
6. I know for sure that I am going to Heaven so I don't need church
7. There is nothing at church for me
8. The Bible doesn't say that I need to go to church
9. The Preacher talks too long
10. The people are unfriendly
11. The greeters are rude and unkind
12. Church people always look mean; they never smile
13. I don't have transportation to and from church
14. The church only wants my money
15. They didn't come to visit me when I was sick or in the Hospital
16. The Pastor, Deacons and Trustees pocket the money
17. I don't have anything to wear
18. My kids don't have shoes to wear
19. I'm on medication and I have to eat at a certain time
20. They stay in church too long and I have other stuff to do
21. I have to work
22. I don't like crowds
23. I have to cook on Sundays
24. The drums are too loud and I can't hear the preacher
25. People only go to church for a fashion show and to be seen
26. People only go to church to be spectators
27. Church people were in the club last night
28. It's too hot/cold to go to church
29. I joined a church in my home city
30. I don't believe in God
31. The people don't live right, but they try to tell you how to live

32. The men in church are too flirtatious
33. The preacher thinks that he knows it all
34. My son has a baseball game
35. I have to repair and wash my car
36. I have to clean my house
37. I'm burnt out with church
38. I had to go to church everyday growing up so I don't go now
39. I have homework to complete
40. I can't get my children up and dressed on time
41. They won't let me chew my gum or drink inside
42. I went out last night and I don't want to be a hypocrite
43. I got drunk last night and I have a hangover
44. I'm waiting until I get my life together; I'm not living right
45. I've gained too much weight and can't fit in my clothes
46. I don't have money to put in the offering
47. I have to babysit my grandkids
48. It's my only day to sleep in
49. The Preacher hits on all the women in the church
50. Those young girls dress like they are going to a strip club
51. The women want to date the pastor
52. The Deacons smoke cigarettes outside the church
53. They people are fake and sin before they get out of church
54. They're all having affairs with each other's spouse.
55. I don't like the people there
56. The Preacher is always talking about folks' business
57. I don't like the songs they sang
58. They play the music too loud and I get a headache
59. I have a weak bladder: I can't sit too long
60. The seats are too hard
61. I have to go to the restroom often
62. I know some of the people there and I don't like them
63. The church is too big
64. The church is too small

65. *There are too many young people that go there*
66. *The people there are old*
67. *The preacher can't preach well*
68. *I watch church on TV or the internet*
69. *I used to go to church; I don't know why I don't go anymore*
70. *The church has too many cliques*
71. *I was hurt by the church a long time ago*
72. *They wouldn't let me lead any songs in the choir*
73. *No one has ever invited me to church*
74. *They are all hypocrites*
75. *I don't have anyone to go with me*
76. *I was not raised up in church*
77. *I don't have church clothes*
78. *Church makes me nervous*
79. *I don't believe in church*
80. *Church is for girly men*
81. *I have done so much wrong, there's no hope for me*
82. *My spouse won't go to church with me*
83. *My spouse gets upset with me when I go to church*
84. *I suffer with pain in my body and can't sit that long*
85. *I am ashamed of my past; I've made a lot of mistakes*
86. *The people are judgmental*
87. *I don't fit in and the people won't like me*
88. *I'm too depressed to attend church*
89. *I can't find a church here that I like*
90. *I'm not ready yet*
91. *I am dealing with too many problems in my life right now*
92. *I have to clean my house on Sundays*
93. *I am very shy, an introvert and crowds make me nervous*
94. *I read my Bible every day at home*

95. I'm afraid that the preacher will find out that I'm living in sin
96. They dance and shout too much at church
97. My kids are too bad and out of control
98. Church is too commercialized
99. I don't need a preacher to tell me how to life my life.
100 My knees and legs hurt when I stand too long
101 I am not a good person to be around

Conquer with Christ   Marolyn Madison-Evans

101 Reasons why People do go to church

1. The Bible instructs us to assemble together with believers
2. You will have the opportunity to worship God.
3. You will likely have some of life big questions answered.
4. The preaching of the Word will help provide direction for your life.
5. You will make some new friends.
6. You'll probably see some old friends.
7. Being there is a sign of your discipleship.
8. Being there will encourage your family and friends to do likewise.
9. You'll be encouraged in your walk with God.
10. You'll likely encourage other people in their walk with God.
11. If you're single, you may meet someone.
12. It will help you define what you believe.
13. It will help you understand the Bible.
14. If you have kids, it will teach them to value God and His Church.
15. People who attend church usually live longer
16. It will give you an outlet for service and ministry
17. It can help you develop personal leadership.
18. You'll sing inspirational songs that will carry you during the week.
19. It will continue to remind you that God is good
20. It will help you to look outside yourself.
21. It will provide an opportunity to give financially to those in need.
22. You'll receive love from other people.
23. You'll be able to show love   toward others.

24. You'll hear about the great things God is doing in His Church locally and throughout the Earth.

25. You'll be prayed for.

26. You will be able to pray for others.

27. You're likely to hear and be encouraged by answered prayers.

28. You will be able to give praise reports and share stories of God working in your life.

29. You will be able to worship God with other likeminded people.

30. it's an opportunity to introduce a friend who doesn't know Christ.

31. You've probably got nothing better to do. (Watching TV, or sleeping-in don't count as better!)

32. Your family need you to go

33. It honors God.

34. Because gathering is part of what it means to be a Christian.

35. Because it's good to have your views and opinions challenged.

36. Because we all need regular reminders of our position in Christ.

37. It will help you acknowledge and confess your sins.

38. It helps you to be in the world, but not of it.

39. It will help you end one week, and starts the next, with the right focus.

40. It's a break from work.

41. It will help you re-order your priorities.

42. It's where your real friends are.

43. It will help you put your life story, into the grand narrative of scripture.

44. It will remind you that you have nothing to fear.

45. *It helps take your focus off yourself and onto God.*

46. *It helps bring perspective and feeds the soul.*

47. *Because gathering strengthens your faith.*

48. *The discipline of going will help you be disciplined across all areas of life.*

49. *It will allow for support in times of need.*

50. *It promotes stability in your life.*

51. *It helps to promote a happy marriage.*

52. *It gives you something great to do with your kids.*

53. *It will help you to improve your self-esteem.*

54. *It will help your interpersonal skills.*

55. *It will help increase your ability to cope with the trials of life.*

56. *It will help you to be a happy person.*

57. *It will positively influence future generations.*

58. *It will provide you with an opportunity to share in communion.*

59. *It will allow you to take an active role in missions work.*

60. *It will help you be a better member of your local community.*

61. *It will help develop your children's self-confidence.*

62. *Your children will learn the Bible.*

63. *It may keep you out of trouble.*

64. *It will help give you a sense of purpose.*

65. *It will shape your vision of the future.*

66. *It will give you eternal hope.*

67. *It will help you to know what you believe.*

68. *It will help you to know what you stand for.*

69. It will encourage creativity.

70. It will allow you to be disciplined, mentored and pastored.

71. Because you'll learn about Jesus and have the opportunity to get to know Him.

72. Because you want to go.

73. It's a pleasant experience.

74. It will give you the opportunity to express yourself in song.

75. It beats staying at home and being alone.

76. You get to put your Sunday best on... (or your skinny jeans depending on the church).

77. You'll find acceptance.

78. You'll be loved.

79. You can love others there

80. Real forgiveness is found there.

81. The gathering of God's people will help draw you closer to God.

82. You'll meet likeminded people.

83. Jesus will be there.

84. It will remind you that you're not alone.

85. It will help the process of sanctification.

86. You're likely to learn something about God, the Bible, yourself, or others.

87. Growth of the fruit of the Spirit will likely happen.

88. It will bring with it tangible and intangible blessing.

90. It's a declaration that you're a Christian.

91. It gives you something interesting to talk about on Monday at work.

92. *Because being planted will help your life to flourish.*

93. *It reflects a life lived beyond yourself.*

94. *It will bring joy to your life.*

95. *A miracle you need may come to pass.*

96. *You've been promising someone that you'd go and it's time to make good on your word.*

97. *Because it's the right thing to do.*

98. *Because faith without works is dead.*

99. *It will literally change your life for eternity!*

100. *You can share the message with others*

101. *You learn more about religion*

Conquer with Christ   Marolyn Madison-Evans

You are cordially invited to worship with us at Faith Ministries Church in Columbus, Ohio at the following location:

Faith Ministries Church
2747 Agler Road
Columbus, Ohio 43224
614-416-8500
Dr. C. Dexter Wise III, Pastor
Sunday Worship at 10:00am. Tuesday Night Bible Study 7:00pm

Faith Ministries Church

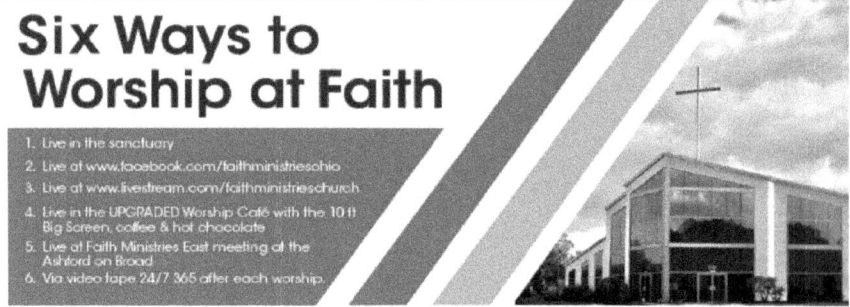

Conquer with Christ   Marolyn Madison-Evans

You are cordially invited to worship with us at the Full Gospel Baptist Church-Five Church Fellowship in Pensacola, Florida at the following locations:

Friendship Missionary Baptist Church
2601 W. Strong Street
Pensacola, Florida 32505
850-439-1080
Pastor, LuTimothy May Sr.
State of Florida FGBCF West District Overseer
Sunday worship at 8:00am & 11:00am. Wednesday Bible Study 7:00pm

St. James Missionary Baptist Church
219 E. Johnson Avenue
Pensacola, Florida 32514
850-476-0690
Pastor, Charles Thomas
Sunday worship at 11:00am. Wednesday Bible Study 7:00pm

Englewood Missionary Baptist Church
1100 W. Scott Street
Pensacola, Florida 32501
850-434-1440
Pastor, Larry Watson, Jr.
Sunday worship at 11:00am. Wednesday Bible Study 7:00pm

Empowerment Church
407 W. Michigan Avenue
Pensacola, Florida 32505
850-466-2523
Pastor, Brian Thompson
Sunday worship at 11:00am. Wednesday Bible Study 7:00pm

Friendship Primitive Baptist Church
1213 W. Blount Street
Pensacola, Florida 32501
850-438-3243
Pastor, Grover Brown, Jr.
Sunday worship at 11:00am. Wednesday Bible Study 7:00pm

A Prayer of Faith: **By Helen Madison**

Father God, in the precious name of Jesus, I come before Your presence today lifting up holy hands and giving you praise, glory and honor for who You are. You are my King, You are my God, You are my peace, You are my power, You are my provision, and You are my everything. You are a God of great possibilities and there is nothing too hard for You. Thank you for forgiving us of all of our sins and for washing us as white as snow. Thank You for making every crocked place straight and the rough places smooth. Thank You for always going before us to lighten our dark path and for going behind us as a shield to comfort, strengthen and protect us. You are our strength and there is non like You. You are a present help in time of need. Thank You for hearing and for answering our prayers. You promised that You would keep us in perfect peace if we keep our minds stayed on You. Thank You for building us up when we are torn down, You strengthen us when we are weak, and You bring comfort when we are discouraged. You are our great physician and You have healed us from all sicknesses and diseases. We say, thank You. Thank You for deliverance and salvation. Thank You that Your promises are yea and amen. Lord, I ask that You will continue to bless my family and families around the world. Remove any evil and wrongdoing from our hearts. Let our speech be edifying, uplifting, and pleasing in Your sight. May we bring glory and honor to Your holy name. Allow us to walk in peace and reject the voice of the adversary so that we may hear from You. Remove the scales from our eyes so that we may see your face. Guide our feet so that we may not stumble but walk with Thee. Bless everything that we set our hands to do. Thank You that You have already given us the VICTORY over our enemies. Thank you that no weapons formed against me and my family, friends and loved ones will be able to prosper and every tongue that rises up against us in judgement will be condemned in the name of Jesus. Isaiah 54:17. I thank You and I give You all the praise, glory and honor in Jesus name I pray. Amen.

References

Abused and Battered Women Facts & Statistics, 2012, www.shimmymob.com/purpose/abuse_facts/.

"Addiction Recovery – Alcohol and Drug Abuse Treatment Resources." *Recovery.org*, Recovery Brands LLC, a Subsidiary of American Addiction Centers, Inc., 27 Apr. 2018, www.recovery.org/.

"Addictions Treatment - Most Trusted for Alcohol Detox and Drug Rehab." *Addictions*, Addictions.com, 11 Sep. 2018, www.addictions.com/.

Adolescents' relationships with peers. In R. M. Lerner & L. Steinberg (Eds.), *Handbook of Adolescent Psychology*, 2nd edition (pp. 363-394) New York; Wiley. Brown, B.B. (2004).

Advanced Solutions International, Inc. "American Association for Marriage and Family Therapy." *Families Living with HIV*, 11 Sep. 2018, www.aamft.org/.

"American Foundation for Suicide Prevention." *AFSP*, Sept. 2018, afsp.org/.

"Childhelp A Non-Profit Charity Aiding Victims of Child Abuse." *Childhelp*, 11 Sep. 2018, www.childhelpusa.com/.

"Christian Counseling Resources You Can Trust...." *Christian Counseling, Scriptures, Counselor Resources, and Treatment*, 11 Sep. 2018, www.counseling4christians.com/.

"Convention on the Elimination of All Forms of Discrimination Against Women." *Wikipedia*, Wikimedia Foundation, 26 Aug. 2018, en.wikipedia.org/wiki/Convention_on_the_Elimination_of_All_Forms_of_Discrimination_Against_Women.

"Courses for Parents and Kids." *Nationwide Children's Hospital*, 11 Sep. 2018, www.NationwideChildrens.org/edu.

"Crime in the U.S. 2007." FBI, FBI, 8 Oct. 2010, ucr.fbi.gov/crime-in-the-u.s/2007.

"Depression." *National Institute of Mental Health*, U.S. Department of Health and Human Services, 2015, www.nimh.nih.gov/health/topics/depression/index.shtml.

Enriching and Equipping Spirit-Filled Ministers." Enrichment Journal, 11 Sep. 2018, www.enrichmentjournal.ag.org/.

"Enrichment Journal - Enriching and Equipping Spirit-Filled Ministers." The Place of Women in the Graeco-Roman World, 11 Sep. 2018, www.enrichmentjournal.ag.org/.

"Find Help Near You En Español." *RAINN | Rape, Abuse and Incest National Network*, 11 Sep. 2018, centers.rainn.org/.

"Find Life Worth Living." *Rogers Behavioral Health*, 11 Sep. 2018, www.rogershospital.org/.

Friendships, cliques, and crowds. In G. R. Adams & M.D. Berzonsky (Eds.) *Blackwell Handbook of Adolescence* (pp. 330-348) Malden, MA: Blackwell Publishing. Steinberg, L. (2006) Adolescence. New York, NY: McGraw-Hill.

"How Will the Uninsured Fare Under the Affordable Care Act?" *The Henry J. Kaiser Family Foundation*, 4 Sept. 2014, www.kff.org/health-reform/fact-sheet/how-will-the-uninsured-fare-under-the-affordable-care-act/. Published: Apr. 7, 2014

"Home." *Lifeline*, 11 Sep. 2018, www.suicidepreventionlifeline.org/.

Jakes, T. D. "He-Motions." *Open Library*, McClure, 2004, openlibrary.org/works/OL57735W/He-Motions.

Kerby, Sophia. "The Top 10 Most Startling Facts About People of Color and Criminal Justice in the United States." *Center for American Progress*, 29 May 2015, www.americanprogress.org/issues/race/news/2012/03/ 13/11351/the-top-10-most-startling-facts-about-people-of-color-and-criminal-justice-in-the-united-states/.

Macer, Karlee, National Association for Female Executives and Women in Networking. *"A World for our Daughters."* Women's History Month, Defense Finance and Accounting Service, CO. 4 March 2013.

"Men's Ministry." *Men's Ministry*, Sept. 2018, men.ag.org/.

"Marriage Fitness with Mort Fertel - Official Web Site - Home Page." Marriage Fitness, 11 Sep. 2018, www.marriagemax.com/.

"Marriage Made EZ in 31 Days." *Amazon*, Amazon, 24 Apr. 2012, www.amazon.com/Marriage-Made-EZ-31-Days/dp/0982818025.

"National Center for Health Statistics." *Centers for Disease Control and Prevention*, Centers for Disease Control and Prevention, 13 Sept. 2018, www.cdc.gov/nchs/index.htm.

NebFact 211"Adolescence and Peer Pressure" by Herbert G. Lingren and the University of Nebraska –*Lincoln Extension Publications* web site on Adolescence and Youth. Aug 2007.

"Need to Talk? We're Here for You." *Adult Survivors of Child Sexual Abuse | RAINN*, 11 Sep. 2018, www.rainn.org/.

Nsopw. "United States Department of Justice National Sex Offender Public Website." *Facts and Statistics*, www.nsopw.gov/en/Education/FactsStatistics?AspxAutoDetectCookieSupport=1. 1997

Peer groups and peer cultures. In S. S. Feldman & G. R. Elliott (Eds.) At the threshold: *The developing adolescent* (pp. 171-198). Cambridge, MA: Harvard University Press. Brown, B.B. (1990)

"Peer Pressure Facts." *Behavior Charts - Reward System for Kids - Parenting | Kid Pointz*, 2015, www.kidpointz.com/parenting-articles/elementary-school/peer-pressure/view/peer-pressure-facts/. 11 Sep. 2018

"Pfizer for Professionals." *Clinical History*, 11 Sep. 2018, www.pfizerpro.com/.

"Sermons and Speeches of Martin Luther King, Jr." *Wikipedia*, Wikimedia Foundation, 19 July 2016, en.wikipedia.org/wiki/Sermons_and_speeches_of_Martin_Luther_King,_Jr.

"StopBullying.gov." *StopBullying.gov*, Department of Health and Human Services, 11 Sep. 2018, www.stopbullying.gov/,

Sutter, John D. "5 Warning Signs of Gaming Addiction." *CNN*, Cable News Network, 6 Aug. 2012, www.cnn.com/2012/08/05/tech/gaming-gadgets/gaming-addiction-warning-signs/index.html.

"Title VII of the Civil Rights Act of 1964." *Information about the Americans with Disabilities Act Amendments Act (ADAAA)*, 2015, www.eeoc.gov/laws/statutes/titlevii.cfm.

Tavernise, Sabrina. "U.S. Suicide Rate Surges to a 30-Year High." *The New York Times*, The New York Times, 22 Apr. 2016, www.nytimes.com/2016/04/22/health/us-suicide-rate-surges-to-a-30-year-high.html.

Topics: Discrimination, Gender Discrimination -- *Women*. "*Prison Legal News.*" Prisoner Organ Transplants, Donations Create Controversy | Prison Legal News, 1999, www.prisonlegalnews.org/news/publications/bojs-women-offenders-1999/.

"Types of Domestic Violence." *WEAVE, Inc.*, 2015, www.weaveinc.org/types-domestic-violence.

"VAWC - Anti Violence against Women and Their Children Act of 2004 (Republic Act 9262)." *LAGMALAW*, 2015, mylawyer.asia/node/40.
"Victims and Perpetrators." *National Institute of Justice*, 11 Sep. 2018, www.nij.gov/topics/crime/rape-sexual-violence/Pages/victims-perpetrators.aspx.

"Victims and Perpetrators." *National Institute of Justice*, www.nij.gov/topics/crime/rape-sexual-violence/Pages/victims-perpetrators.aspx. 2000

"Watermark Dallas." *Watermark*, Sept. 2018, www.watermark.org/dallas/.

About The Author:

Marolyn D. Madison-Evans was born on May 6, 1961 in Pensacola, Florida. She has one son, Alan V. Evans and twin grandsons, Ali C. Evans and Aki C. Evans. On August 3, 2016 Marolyn retired as a senior accountant and a Department of Defense certified financial manager-Level 2 with The Under Secretary of Defense (Comptroller) while assigned to the Audit Assertion Branch with The Defense Finance and Accounting Service, Co. after 37 years of service. Marolyn received her Associate of Science degree in stenography in 1984 from Pensacola State College and graduated at top of her class as Magna Cum Laude with dual Bachelor of Science degrees in Management/Accounting and Management in 2015 from Park University. In October 2013-2014, Marolyn attended the Wise School of Ministry, Columbus, Ohio, where Dr. C. Dexter Wise, III is the founding President, and received a certificate of completion in basic and intermediate biblical studies. She is currently enrolled in leadership classes at Friendship Missionary Baptist Church, Pensacola, Florida where Lutimothy May, Sr. is the residing Pastor. She is an educator with the Escambia County Public school system in Pensacola, Florida. She is an author and publisher. She enjoys reading, writing, traveling and spending time with family.

Conquer with Christ   Marolyn Madison-Evans

For additional copies of this book or to book a speaking engagement with Marolyn, you may contact the author/publisher at the following location:

Marolyn Madison-Evans
P.O. Box 18223
Pensacola, Florida 32523-8223
www.marolynevans.com
marolynevans@gmail.com

Like us on Facebook, Instagram, and Twitter

Conquer with Christ   Marolyn Madison-Evans

www.ingramcontent.com/pod-product-compliance
Lightning Source LLC
LaVergne TN
LVHW051606070426
835507LV00021B/2793